CW00920311

Decolonizing Sociology

Decolonizing the Curriculum

Ali Meghji: *Decolonizing Sociology*
Robbie Shilliam: *Decolonizing Politics*

Decolonizing Sociology

An Introduction

Ali Meghji

polity

First published in 2021 by Polity Press

Polity Press
65 Bridge Street
Cambridge CB2 1UR, UK

Polity Press
101 Station Landing
Suite 300
Medford, MA 02155, USA

ISBN-13: 978-1-5095-4194-2
ISBN-13: 978-1-5095-4195-9 (pb)

A catalogue record for this book is available from the British Library.

Library of Congress Cataloging-in-Publication Data
Names: Meghji, Ali, author.
Title: Decolonizing sociology : an introduction / Ali Meghji.
Description: Cambridge, UK ; Medford, MA : Polity Press, 2020. | Includes
    bibliographical references and index. | Summary: "An action plan for a
    globally equitable sociology"-- Provided by publisher.
Identifiers: LCCN 2020023850 (print) | LCCN 2020023851 (ebook) | ISBN
    9781509541942 (hardback) | ISBN 9781509541959 (paperback) | ISBN
    9781509541966 (epub)
Subjects: LCSH: Sociology--Philosophy. | Postcolonialism. | Racism in
    sociology
Classification: LCC HM435 .M45 2020 (print) | LCC HM435 (ebook) | DDC
    301.01--dc23
LC record available at https://lccn.loc.gov/2020023850
LC ebook record available at https://lccn.loc.gov/2020023851

Typeset in 10.5 on 12pt Sabon
by Fakenham Prepress Solutions, Fakenham, Norfolk NR21 8NL
Printed and bound in Great Britain by CPI Group (UK) Ltd, Croydon

For further information on Polity, visit our website:
politybooks.com

Contents

Acknowledgements

As I read through the pages of this book, I am reminded of numerous conversations about decolonial sociology that I have had with friends, colleagues and students. As usual, I owe thanks to many people from my institution at the University of Cambridge, including members of our Decolonizing Sociology working group such as Dr Mónica Moreno Figueroa, Dr Manali Desai, Dr Tiffany Page, Dr Ella McPherson, Dr Kathryn Medien, Dr Jeff Miley and Professor Sarah Franklin. Each of these scholars has helped develop dialogues around coloniality and sociology, and has helped sustain an engaging intellectual community dedicated to making sociology a more critical, equitable discipline. Of course, this intellectual community was not composed just of those employed as academics, but also copious numbers of students with a deep passion for generating critical sociological knowledge. My thanks go to each of these students, as well as all of the undergraduate and graduate students I have taught who have equally taught me about decolonial sociology. Also at Cambridge, the co-convenors of the Black Radicalism research group – including Dr Tanisha Spratt, Dr Rachell Sánchez-Rivera, Dr Daphne Martschenko and Sharon Walker – also helped inspire understandings of transnational anti-colonial thought and practice. My understanding of transnational links between anti-racist and anti-colonial movements across the world was also furthered when I had the pleasure of co-interviewing Angela Davis when she visited Cambridge.

Outside of my institution, there are a range of people who have helped shape this book. Several years ago, Professor Gurminder K. Bhambra keynoted at a conference I organized on 'Social theory beyond whiteness'. Gurminder's presentation deepened my interest in inequality and canon formation in sociology, and her work continues to be a reference point for my understanding of why we need a decolonial sociology, and what this sociology ought to look like. With Gurminder, I am a co-convenor of the British Sociological Association's Post/decolonial Transformations working group, along with Dr Sara Salem, Dr Meghan Tinsley and Saskia Papadakis. Each of these intellectuals is pushing the boundaries of sociology in their work, and has helped instil a decolonial spirit into British and international academia. A close friend and collaborator, Dr Rima Saini, is also developing debates over decoloniality and curriculum reform in the social sciences, and I thank her for stimulating conversations as well as constant support.

Of course, the decolonial spirit is one which rejects hierarchies in favour of collaboration and conversation. I was fortunate enough to be on the receiving end of this spirit of kindness as I was forming the arguments of this book. While at Harvard, Professor Julian Go kindly made the time to have coffee with me, and helped provide advice on how a decolonial sociology is much more than an issue of 'race'; this was a watershed moment for me in my understanding of decolonial sociology. At the same time, conversations with Professor Michèle Lamont helped me to deepen my understanding of social theory, the sociology of valuation and canon formation. While visiting Cambridge, Professor Raewyn Connell also made the time to have coffee with me, providing me not only with an endless list of references to follow up, but also with explicit advice on how to write a 'review' book; again, I am indebted to this help. On the theme of help, I also owe thanks to Professors Les Back and Satnam Virdee. Before my interest in decoloniality I was primarily a sociologist of race, and both Les and Satnam helped me to see how race scholarship in the United Kingdom was often formed around the principles of anti-imperial, decolonial sociology. I also owe thanks to mentors such as Professors John Solomos and Derron Wallace, both of whom are incredibly kind and supportive. Of course, I also owe a significant deal to the editorial team at Polity – especially Jonathan Skerrett and Karina Jákupsdóttir. Karina helped gather incredibly helpful reviews on drafts of my manuscript, while Jonathan's editorial comments greatly improved this manuscript's clarity. Both Jonathan and Karina played a central role in developing this from a book proposal to a completed manuscript.

Lastly, I thank my partner, Emily Chan, and the newest addition to our family – Maisie. Emily is loving, supportive, affectionate, and provides constant encouragement. She is my rock and foundation, and brings me constant happiness and joy.

Thank you, everybody.

Introduction: Sociology and Coloniality

As someone interested in decolonial theory, I often find myself reflecting on my relationship with sociology. I did not study sociology until part way through my undergraduate degree, and in this regard, I was never formally introduced to the works of Karl Marx, Max Weber or Émile Durkheim. Not having sat down and systematically read Marx, Weber and Durkheim became a secret of mine that I kept close to my chest at the beginning of graduate school. Readers of this book will be pleased to know that since then I have become acquainted with such 'classical' works, but it remains puzzling that three figures, two of whom did not even classify themselves as sociologists, and none of whom were regarded as sociologists by their contemporaries (Connell 1997), have come to hold so much symbolic weight in the field of sociology. Now as an advisor, I regularly get graduate students – much less secretive than I was – declaring anxieties to me that they aren't familiar with the works of Marx, Weber and Durkheim, questioning whether that makes them 'bad sociologists'.

How have we got to the point where students see it as a moral obligation to read Marx, Weber and Durkheim? How have we got to the point where those who are not familiar with these three thinkers are construed as having some form of sociological deficiency? Why is the sociological canon composed as it is, and what does this tell us about the dominant vision of sociology? Do we even need a socio- logical canon? This book reflects on some of these questions throughout the following chapters. However, in order to fully understand the responses to these questions, and consequently to tackle the wider problem of 'decolonizing' sociology, we need to situate the development of sociology in its proper colonial history. This is because, although we are regularly presented with a picture of sociology as being one of the most 'critical' of the social sciences, sociology became formally institutionalized in the nineteenth century at the height of global colonialism, imperialism and empires. This world of colonialism and empires was not merely background noise to sociology, but rather the discipline came to internalize colonial ways of thinking and representing the world. Over a century later, and this colonial style of knowledge production still shapes sociological practice. In this regard, actions for the future of sociology require a significant examination of the discipline's past.

Sociology, colonialism and colonial difference

Sociology is unlike many of the other disciplines covered in Polity's 'Decolonizing the Curriculum' series – including philosophy, history, natural science, music, theology, economics and English literature – in that sociology did not have a formal existence before European colonialism. While people were certainly *thinking* sociologically for a very long time, in terms of being a formal academic discipline with institutional recognition, sociology did not arrive on the academic scene until the nineteenth century at the high point of colonialism. Thus, speaking about the US, Julian Go (2016a) points out that the first sociology PhD awarded in the US – William Fremont Blackman's *The Making of Hawaii* – was published in 1893, the same year that the US overthrew the Hawaiian monarchy. Go (2016a) additionally points out that as the first school of sociology in the US was set up in Chicago in 1893, France was colonizing the

Ivory Coast, Laos and Guinea, and as the first issue of the *American Journal of Sociology* was published in 1895, the Cuban rebellion against the Spanish began. Outside of the US, we may add that the first sociology department set up in the UK, in 1904 at the London School of Economics, was established the same year that we see the first genocide of the twentieth century (the Herero and Nama genocide conducted by the German empire), while the first sociology department set up in mainland Europe (in Bordeaux, 1895) happened in the same year that French West Africa was founded. Simply put, sociology formally developed in a world that was shaped by the processes of colonialism and empire.

In terms of decolonizing sociology, unlike many other disciplines, therefore, sociology did not 'become' colonized; rather, it was always colonial to begin with. By saying that sociology was colonial, I mean that sociology both internalized the logic of a colonial episteme, and also (re)-produced and bolstered that very episteme itself. Epistemes are ways of thinking and knowing, they set the limits of what can be known, as well as dictating what counts as legitimate knowledge and how this knowledge can be legitimately produced (Meghji 2019a). When speaking of a colonial episteme, therefore, I am referring to dominant ways of thinking and knowing that produced and reproduced *colonial difference*: the idea that the colonized were inherently different from (and inferior to) the Western colonizers.

One of the paradoxes of world history, as Gurminder K. Bhambra (2014: 132) states, is that 'colonization invent[ed] the colonized'. What is evoked in Bhambra's statement is a recognition of the interplay between power, knowledge (epistemology) and being (ontology), and how the imbalances of power created in colonialism had epistemic-ontological dimensions. The idea that colonized people were inherently different from the colonized was not a 'given' fact, but was a form of knowledge that had to be actively produced by colonial empires (Mignolo 2012). The creation of race, as a master-category through which we could categorize the world's population, was a primary mechanism through which colonial difference could be made (Mills 1997). Thus, through the concept of race in the sixteenth century, Spanish colonizers were able to draw links between the indigenous people's[1] *raza* (blood) and their being *gente sin razón* (people without reason) (Lewis 2012), while the biological revolution in the eighteenth century allowed for a more rigid conception of race that held non-white racialized groups as naturally inferior to whites (Banton and Harwood 1975). The concept of race was thus the glue that stuck the colonial world order together, as it became common-sense knowledge that there was a global racial hierarchy which permitted the colonization of the 'lesser' races by the dominant white Europeans. This global hierarchy is well described by W. E. B. Du Bois (1967 [1899]: 386–7) when he comments:

> We grant full citizenship in the World Commonwealth to the 'Anglo-Saxon' (whatever that may mean), the Teuton and the Latin; then with just a shade of reluctance we extend it to the Celt and Slav. We half deny it to the yellow races of Asia, admit the brown Indians to an ante-room only on the strength of an undeniable past; but with the Negroes of Africa we come to a full stop, and in its heart the civilized world with one accord denies that these come within the pale of nineteenth-century Humanity.

What is captured in Du Bois' remark is that colonial difference divided the world through the taxonomy of race. However, this division of the world was not just geographical, and did not aim to just specify where the 'different races' of the world lived. Rather, the colonial difference that ruptured the world also asserted that people in different regions across the world were in different temporal stages of human development, and consequently had essential ontological differences; scholars have referred to these processes as the coloniality of time (Demuro 2015; Mignolo 2012) and the coloniality of being (Maldonado-Torres 2017; Wynter 2003).

In terms of the *coloniality of time*, the 'myth' of colonial difference relied upon the premise that the colonized were less developed – as a civilization – than those living in the

West (Mignolo 2012; Mills 2014). It was this very logic that allowed colonial empires to justify their actions on the pretence of 'bringing civilization' to the rest of the world, and indeed, this temporal grammar is still used in the present day when we continue to refer to the 'undeveloped' regions of the world (rather than, as scholars such as Walter Rodney (2018 [1972]) have argued, using the term 'underdeveloped', which stresses the overdevelopment of the West through colonialism). In terms of the *coloniality of being*, as Sylvia Wynter (2003) argues, colonial difference relied on the premise that only the white Westerners achieved the full status of 'man', while the colonized people of the world were all varying degrees of sub-human. Overt examples of this may include the evolutionist idea that Black people were closer to animals than mankind, as analysed by Wulf Hund (2015), and the way that colonized people throughout the world were referred to as savages. Indeed, it was through the coloniality of being that imperial powers could support liberal legislation 'at home' while still exploiting people in their colonies. For instance, France's 1789 Declaration of the Rights of Man and of the Citizen claimed that there are certain universal rights to be protected for all people, and yet at the same time France was running a murderous empire (Wilder 2004). As Charles W. Mills (1997) thus points out, colonizers across the world could defend themselves as liberal because colonized people were not considered fully human, so did not qualify under the supposedly universal laws protecting the rights of 'man'; *justice* thus became a resource for *just-us*.

With colonialism, starting in the sixteenth century, therefore, the world became epistemically, ontologically and temporally divided and hierarchically organized, in what Aníbal Quijano (2007) has referred to as the *colonial matrix of power*. It is now a fairly common view held in the sociology of knowledge that academic disciplines are not impervious to the 'outside world', and, indeed, are often shaped by the external world.[2] Thus, if sociology developed in this world marked by the colonial matrix of power, surely it is apt to assume that sociology itself was in some ways influenced by this world. In fact, when we actually look at the development of sociology in the nineteenth and twentieth centuries, we see that sociology was a key academic discipline in producing and reproducing colonial difference. One of the first missions for 'decolonizing' sociology, therefore, involves what George Steinmetz (2017) refers to as a disciplinary remembering, where we can show that sociology both internalized the colonial episteme, and continues to be shaped by this episteme in the present day. This disciplinary remembering, however, requires us to tell quite a different story of sociology's past and present from what we regularly encounter in our textbooks and classrooms. It is useful to begin by considering sociology's development in the metropoles – the imperial centres of the colonizing world.

Imperialism, colonialism, empire: While these three processes are often interlinked, Steinmetz's (2014) general division between the three is helpful. Empires are political organizations 'that significantly limit the sovereignty of the peoples and polities they conquer', while imperialism is a 'strategy of political control over foreign lands that does not necessarily involve conquest, occupation, and durable rule by outside invaders' (Steinmetz 2014: 79). On the other hand, with colonialism, we have 'the conquest of a foreign people followed by the creation of an organization controlled by members of the conquering polity and suited to rule over the conquered territory's indigenous population. [...] Colonialism always involves the arrogation of sovereignty by a conquering power, whose rule is presented as permanent' (Steinmetz 2014: 79).

Metropole: Metropoles are the nucleus, the 'home cities' of empires. London was thus the metropole of the British empire, just as Paris was of the French empire. Sociologists have found it useful to use the notion of metropoles to highlight how Western sociologists were producing knowledge not in a nationally isolated world, but in fact in the epicentre of a world globally connected through colonialism (Connell 1997).

Sociology in the metropoles

There are sometimes tendencies, even within decolonial schools of thought, to assume that sociology began in the nineteenth century as a discipline involving European thinkers discussing European societies.[3] However, as shown by recent revisionist historians of sociology, as sociology developed within Europe and the US in the nineteenth century, sociologists were deeply interested in issues pertaining to empires and colonialism.[4] In fact, even the supposedly 'first' European thinker to use the term 'sociology' – Auguste Comte (2009 [1853]) in his *Cours de philosophie positive* – dedicated a section of his book to the discussion of the pros and cons of colonial rule, concluding that colonialism was 'a social monstrosity' (175), and that

> It is not our business to decide by anticipation what that preparatory course must be, nor when it shall terminate; nor to suppose that each race or nation must imitate in all particulars the mode of progression of those which have gone before. Except for the maintenance of general peace, or the natural extension of industrial relations, Western Europe must avoid any large political intervention in the East. (491)[5]

Indeed, as Go (2009: 778) shows, in the *American Journal of Sociology* (*AJS*) 'the percentage of articles [...] that referred to "empires", 'imperialism", "colonies", or "colonialism" from 1895 to 1914 had a mean of 36 percent. [...] In 1902, the percentage of articles that referred to those keywords reached as high as 60 percent.' Further, not only were the topics of empires, colonialism and imperialism featuring in the *AJS*, but US-based sociologists saw these processes as *key* topics of investigation. In his presidential address to the American Sociological Association, for instance, Franklin Giddings (1911: 580–1) went as far as to say that 'questions of territorial expansion and of rule over alien peoples' were the most important issue for sociologists to study. Even the sociologists now renowned for their analyses of US society were in fact more interested in global processes in their early writings. Robert Park, for instance, is renowned for his studies of 'race relations' in Chicago, but prior to his interests in US urban sociology, Park was interested in much more global issues, including the role of Europe in 'uplifting' the African continent through colonialism (Magubane 2013).

From the nineteenth century until the post-war period, colonialism and empire were thus the hot topics for sociologists, with most of the 'founding fathers' of US sociology teaching courses on these processes (Go 2016a). A dominant argument in revisionist histories of sociology, as offered by Raewyn Connell (1997) among others, is that after World War II, US sociology became a lot more inward-looking – largely limiting itself to the study of US society – while European sociology (and particularly British sociology) came to import this 'new' insular US sociology, particularly the structural functionalism paradigm pioneered by Talcott Parsons. However, if we look at British sociology as a case, then we can see how the socio-logical interest in colonialism and imperialism was preserved far into the post-war period (despite little mention of this in recent histories of British sociology[6]). From the archives of *The British Journal of Sociology* (*BJS*), for instance, we can see that in the post-war period, British sociologists were interested in issues including marriage patterns across Africa (Leach 1953), colonial resistance in South Africa (Kuper 1953), how to strengthen British colonial administration (Friedman 1951), the value of 'colour' in Jamaica (Henriques 1951) and the ethnic demography of East Africa (Sofer and Ross 1951), among many other topics.

It seems, therefore, that from Comte's discussion of 'sociology' in the mid-nineteenth century, well into the disci-pline's next one hundred years of development, sociology had a fixation on colonialism, empires and imperialism. Through engaging with these topics, sociology became a key discipline in producing and reproducing colonial difference. In particular, I think it is useful to see three discrete, although connected, ways that sociologists worked to reproduce colonial difference.

1. Sociologists reproducing the 'civilizational backwardness' thesis

As aforementioned, one key premise of colonial difference was the idea that the colonized were undeveloped sub-persons (contrasted to the 'civilized' European). It was this logic that allowed colonial powers to justify their actions as being part of an overall 'civilizing mission'.[7]

Sociologists not only bought into this myth of colonial difference, but also were committed to buttressing it. We can see this even in the writings of one of the members of the 'holy trinity' of the sociological canon – Durkheim. Durkheim is regularly taught as one of the leading canonical thinkers in sociology, along with Marx and Weber, with particular attention being paid to his critique of Western modernity.[8] The teaching of Durkheim often revolves around his ideas of the societal evolution from mechanical into organic solidarity, as primitive societies become 'advanced' (Durkheim 1997 [1893]). However, Durkheim's typologies of primitive and advanced societies is primarily based on his comparative fieldwork between Aboriginal people in Australia and indigenous Americans, on the one hand, and European societies, on the other (see Kurasawa 2013). In this respect, in order to contrast 'past', 'historic', pre-modern societies with advanced societies, instead of actually consulting history, Durkheim studied colonized people in his present day. As Connell (1997) argues, it was this logic that allowed Durkheim, in his description of mechanical solidarity and primitive societies, to discuss the ancient Hebrews along with the contemporary French colony of Kabylia, without drawing any conceptual distinction between the two cases. The colonized were thus treated as 'the past in the present', as Durkheim and his French contemporaries at *L'Année Sociologique*[9] were able to construct their sociological models around the idea of colonial difference. Further, Durkheim and his French contemporaries were far from being the only sociologists who saw the colonized as 'the past in the present'. Even prior to Durkheim's work, in Britain, Herbert Spencer (2010 [1895]) was already publishing evolutionist ideas in his theory of militant versus industrial society (a similar typology to Durkheim's primitive versus modern societies). As Connell (1997, 2010) shows, Spencer was identical to Durkheim in the way that those in the supposedly historical 'militant' societies were in fact the colonized in the present. In Spencer's (2010 [1895]) sociological exposition, therefore, in order to define militant, primitive societies, he uses a range of colonial examples from Bengal, Tasmania, Victoria and South India.

Across the pond in the US, sociologists were replicating these very same ideas. Take, for instance, Albert Keller's (1906) 'The Value of the Study of Colonies for Sociology'. In this paper, Keller puts forward the idea that colonies are ideal sociological laboratories because they provide us with data on what modern societies *used to be like*.[10] As Keller (1906: 417) states, the 'study of such societies gives us our only starting-points for the scientific demonstration of the evolution of human institutions'. Keller was of the belief that in order for sociology to understand the complexity of the modern world, it must first provide a framework for society in its simplest form. The colonies, to Keller (1906: 418), provided such a pool of data for these 'simple' societies: 'What the sociologist may note with safety is that in the colonial or frontier society there occurs an elimination of many artificial or cultural conditions of life prevalent in the metropolis, and that this results in an approach, more or less close, to conditions of existence characteristic of "savage" societies.' In a similar line of thought, in his 'Standpoint for the Interpretation of Savage Society', W. I. Thomas (1909: 146) states that 'tribal society is virtually delayed civilization, and the savages are a sort of contemporaneous ancestry'. Thomas (1909: 146) thus argued that if sociology is to be a science of man, it should concern itself not only with findings in biology (i.e. biological evolutionary theory), but also with anthropology and ecology, given that 'the lessons which the sciences dealing with man in historical time have to learn from the life of the lower human races are even more important than those which they have learned from biology'. It was only through understanding the 'institutional life of savage society' – through studying the colonies – that sociologists, according to Thomas (1909: 147), were able to understand present modern societies. Early sociologists, therefore, reaped great benefits from colonialism and empire, as the whole colonized world was treated as a pool from which to gather sociological data. As Connell (2010: 41) aptly puts it, to sociologists:

> The colonized world, seen from the metropole, was a magnificent museum of primitiveness [...] the colonized world offered a gallery of social forms, social customs, social groups. Theorists in the metropole could, and did, array these data in a grid of race, levels of economic development, social integration or whatever principle of classification took their fancy. [...] These cultures were, in their eyes, of interest precisely because they were more primitive, representing (as they thought) earlier stages of social development.

Furthermore, it should come as little surprise that some sociologists straightforwardly adopted the 'civilizational backwardness' thesis of colonial difference. Even though sociology was becoming formally institutionalized as a specific discipline in the nineteenth and twentieth centuries, in this period sociology only had a relative autonomy from other disciplines. In Britain, for instance, both Sujata Patel (2010) and Steinmetz (2017) point out that sociology and anthropology were closely related, with many anthropologists publishing in journals such as *The British Journal of Sociology* and *The Sociological Review*. Of course, given that anthropology was one of the key academic institutions used to gather data on the colonized's lifeworlds, cultures and customs, it is clear to see how this anthropological way of thinking came to influence sociology's own dispositions (Huizer and Mannheim 1979; Patel 2010). Similarly in the US, there was a close relationship between political science and sociology in the early twentieth century (Go 2014). While this link may appear to be quite appropriate, we also have to contextualize that this was a period of time when the leading political science journal was called *The Journal of Race Development*, and featured papers such as Ellsworth Huntington's (1914: 185) 'The Adaptability of the White Man to Tropical America', where he argues that:

> The tropical portions of America and Africa, as every one knows, are the richest unexploited regions in the world. If ever they are to be developed the work must apparently be done by people of European origin, for the native races seem incapable of doing it alone, and Europe and America are scarcely willing to leave the task to Asiatics. Yet in spite of innumerable attempts during the past four hundred years the problem of the adaptation of the white races to a tropical environment still remains one of the most serious that has ever confronted mankind. Shall the white man forever be an outsider, a mere exploiter, or shall he become a permanent denizen of the regions which he develops.

Even the link between sociology and political science, therefore, allowed for the exchange and influence of colonial modes of thinking.

Lastly, sociology also only had a relative autonomy from the natural sciences. Indeed, some of the early sociologists also worked as natural scientists: Patrick Geddes in Britain, for instance, not only was a sociologist but also worked as a botanist and zoologist; Herbert Spencer too was a biologist; and Lester Ward, in the US, was a botanist as well as a sociologist. Even sociologists who did not work in the natural sciences still adopted the idea that sociology somehow 'evolved' from (and therefore maintained strong epistemic links with) biology and physics.[11] This link between the social and natural sciences meant that someone like Francis Galton (a leading figure in European eugenics) was able to publish his paper 'Eugenics: Its Definition, Scope, and Aims' (Galton 1904) in the *American Journal of Sociology*. Given sociology's close connection with the natural sciences, it therefore became easy for the idea of a natural, biological, scientifically based racial hierarchy to become a common-sense idea within dominant sociology (Bonilla-Silva 2017). Linnaeus and Darwin – two of the key thinkers behind this idea of a natural racial hierarchy – are thus listed as key influencers for sociologists by Thomas (1896); other sociologists including Spencer (2010 [1895]) in Britain and Gumplowicz (1883) in Germany, and their US-based disciples such as Barnes (1919), Simons (1901), Weatherly (1911) and Ward (1903, 1907, 1913), all invoked the Darwinian concept of survival of the fittest to discuss variations of a global 'race struggle'.

Given that many sociologists clearly endorsed the premise of the colonized's civilizational backwardness, it is no surprise that such sociologists therefore were in favour of colonialism and imperialism. Such sociologists, in this case, were merely replicating the larger colonial logic that it was the duty of the West to bring civilization to the rest of the backward world (Du Bois 2008 [1920]). This feeds into the second way that sociologists worked to produce and reproduce colonial difference: endorsing 'democratic imperialism'.

2. Endorsing democratic imperialism

Colonial difference did not just produce myths and knowledge about the colonized, but also produced myths and knowledge about the colonizer. While the colonized were assumed to be 'backward', the 'West' positioned itself as the beacon of civilization. Through this binary, the myth was able to be produced that the 'West', as the civilized agents of the world, had a *moral* duty to bring their civilization to the rest of the globe.[12] As with the construction of race, this myth of moral obligation started with deeply theological roots, with both Spanish and British colonists seeing empire as bringing salvation to indigenous peoples.[13] However, the metropoles' belief in their moral duty to civilize the rest of the globe was not only grounded in theology, but also took on economic meanings (improving the economic development of the colonies) and cultural meanings (improving the cultural institutions of the colonies). Certain sociologists, sharing in the colonial episteme, supported the belief in this moral duty of the West to uplift the rest, and in doing so, endorsed the idea and possibility of democratic imperialism.

Perhaps one of the most explicit formulations of democratic imperialism from a sociologist comes from Franklin Giddings. In his paper 'Imperialism?', Giddings (1898: 600) stated that colonial (or imperial) rule was an essential process in order for Western nations to continue their economic development:

> the task of governing from a distance the inferior races of mankind will be one of great difficulty – one that will tax every resource of intellect and character; but it is one that must be faced and overcome, if the civilized world is not to abandon all hope of continuing its economic conquest of the natural resources of the globe.

Using the precise example of the US empire, Giddings (1898: 588–9) comments:

> We must find new opportunities for making fortunes by jobs and government contracts. The reservations allotted to our unhappy red men have nearly all been appropriated by rough-riders, and we naturally turn to the sunny lands and gentle savages of Hawaii and Luzon for further practice of the Christian art of exploitation [...] Honolulu may not be as good a field for political banking as Philadelphia has been; and Cuba does not afford unlimited opportunities for the development of Star Route postal facilities. Nevertheless, they offer something better than an honest living, earned in the sweat of one's brow.

Underlying Giddings' reasoning, therefore, was the belief that economic expansion and growth can only be achieved through imperial or colonial control. Furthermore, Giddings did not even see this imperialism as being a necessary evil for such economic development, but argued that there was a consistency between empire and democracy. This logical consistency is later defended by Giddings (1901: 3) in his book *Democracy and Empire*, where he uses the example of the US and British empires to show that while 'both have been continually extending their territorial boundaries, absorbing outlying states or colonial possessions, and developing a complicated system of general or imperial administration [...] the coexistence of democracy and empire has become an approximately perfect blending'. Staying with the example of the British empire, Giddings' (1901: 3) argument was not only that the 'nucleus' of the empire (i.e. England) was becoming increasingly democratic, but also that the British were spreading out this democracy to their colonies and territories; as he states, this was true of Canada and Australia and 'though not quite so obvious [...] it is becoming true of India, of the African colonies, and of the lesser dependencies'.

To Giddings, the British and US empires were examples of 'modern empires'. These modern empires were benevolent in their rule, bringing democracy to the world, and permitting diversities in different people's beliefs and religious practices. The only precursor to this supposed benevolence (although it is not noted as a precursor by Giddings) is that 'as long as they [the colonies] conform to the English sense of the sacredness of life, and to the English requirement of social order, England is willing to respect their local customs' (Giddings 1901: 4). Giddings (1901: 12) concludes that democratic imperialism only works if the colonies accept a 'common loyalty to certain common interests and fundamental principles', but given that these 'common interests' and 'fundamental principles' are defined by the rulers, the extent to which democracy is really in action is doubtful. Indeed, the actions of the British empire – from the Boer concentration camps set up in 1900–2 (the very period Giddings was writing his defence of democratic imperialism) through to the Bengal famine of 1943 and the brutal response to the Mau Mau rebellion in the 1950s – show that democracy was quite far off the agenda.

Despite the fact that empires across the world relied on murderous violence in order to persevere, Giddings was not the only seminal sociologist who supported a version of benign imperialism. In fact, one of the most regularly cited and taught sociologists – Karl Marx – was also in on the act. Of course, it is unfair to state that Marx unequivocally supported imperialism; Kevin Anderson (2010), for instance, has shown how some of Marx's later journalistic writing and thoughts on revolution gave especial praise to anti-imperialism in Ireland. However, as Bhambra (2007) argues, the main undercurrents of Marx's intellectual corpus revolve around the belief in the colonized world being backward, and in need of an uplift into modernity through a revolution which capitalism can offer. Writing specifically on British colonial rule in India, for instance, Marx was of the view that colonialism may have some downfalls, but it is to be praised for the way it has put India on the track to economic development. Marx (1853) argues that 'whatever may have been the crimes of England she was the unconscious tool of history in bringing about' India's economic development, given that:

English interference having placed the spinner in Lancashire and the weaver in Bengal, or sweeping away both Hindoo spinner and weaver, dissolved these small semi-barbarian, semi-civilized communities, by blowing up their economical basis, and thus produced the greatest, and to speak the truth, the only social revolution ever heard of in Asia.

Of course, British colonialism, if anything, prevented an economic revolution given that, as Utsa Patnaik (2017) shows in her critique of the colonial 'drain', over £9 billion worth of capital was stolen from India and channelled into the British economy between 1765 and 1938. Such analysis, however, is occluded from Marx's vision, as he adopts a similar standpoint to Giddings' view that imperialism can help economic prosperity. This standpoint was also a feature of Robert Park's more globally oriented sociology, as critiqued by Zine Magubane (2013). As Magubane shows, Park (1912) was of the belief that colonialism – albeit a more benign one – might be the only way to uplift Black Africa. Park (1906: 353) thus argued that 'Africa must expect to serve a long and hard apprenticeship to Europe, an apprenticeship not unlike that which Negroes in America underwent in slavery', arguing in another paper that 'if the White man and his civilization is to rule the world his government must not be an oppression, the domination of mere stupidity and brute force but a control based on sympathy and understanding' (Park 1906: 353). Of course, given Park's support for and collaboration with violent colonial regimes in Congo and South Africa (Magubane 2013), it may be fair to say that his idea of what a 'control based on sympathy and understanding' involves may be brought into question.

Indeed, Park was only one of many sociologists to have close relationships with colonial administrations. Investigating the role of sociologists in being 'active agents' of colonial control is therefore necessary, and is the next way we can see sociologists reproducing colonial difference.

3. Being active agents of empire

By 'active agents of empire', I am referring either to sociologists whose work was explicitly invoked in colonial administrations, or sociologists who directly worked with colonial administrations. Of course, as Go (2016a) remarks, it is both unfair and inaccurate to assert that all classical sociologists were active agents of empires. Nevertheless, we do also need to appreciate the existence of sociologists who were supporting colonial administrations. Go's examples of this include Durkheim and Comte, both of whom directly or indirectly buttressed French colonial rule. Despite being a critic of colonialism, for example, Comte's positivist social science was explicitly invoked by French colonial administrators in justifying their rule over 'primitive', 'fanatic' Muslims (Amster 2013). Needless to say, the story runs much deeper than two French sociologists.

It was perhaps in Britain that the relationship between sociology and colonial administrations was most formalized. Indeed, one of the first sociologists in Britain – Patrick Geddes – also worked as a colonial town planner, designing towns in India and Palestine (Meller 2005). While Geddes was thus critical of colonialism, he nevertheless partook in forming its physical apparatus. Of the two first sociology professors in Britain, while Leonard Hobhouse was a critic of imperial rule, Edward Westermarck, at the London School of Economics focused his work on the benefits and value of sociology to officials in the colonies (see Steinmetz 2013). This relationship between sociologists and colonial administrations then accelerated in the 1940s and post-war years, as Britain sought to move towards (in British eyes) a more benign form of colonial rule. Thus, the sociologist Raymond Firth, who later became secretary to Britain's Colonial Social Science Research Council (CSSRC), told the British colonial office in 1944 that *The Sociological Review* journal was publishing the material most valuable for understanding the colonies (Steinmetz 2013). Between 1944 and 1961, the CSSRC aimed to fund research that would create a group of social scientists 'versed in colonial problems', therefore enabling research for colonial development (Steinmetz 2013). By 1951, the CSSRC had a sizeable budget, totalling £325,000 over five years, and as Steinmetz (2013) shows, the majority of this funding went to studies which fell under the banner of sociology. Indeed, aside from the CSSRC, the British colonial office also instigated the Devonshire system, which sought to formally train colonial military personnel and civil servants in sociology at universities such as the London School of Economics and the London School of Oriental and Asian Studies (Steinmetz 2017). Such universities thus offered courses on 'social administration' and on the 'application of British social policy and institutions to colonial conditions' (Steinmetz 2013: 372).

While sociologists being active agents of empires was certainly not as common as sociologists theorizing democratic imperialism, or reproducing the 'civilizational backwardness' thesis, it certainly was in the background of the discipline's emergence in the nineteenth and twentieth centuries. Once again, we ought not to be surprised by this process. The world sociologists were working in was a world of colonialism, imperialism and empires. The sociologists acting as 'agents of empires' were thus partaking in what they saw as a usual political apparatus, in the same way that contemporary sociologists may work with industry or the third sector.

Why does this matter? From colonialism to coloniality

Sceptical readers may now be questioning 'So far, you've really only talked about the past of sociology. What relevance does this have for decolonizing sociology *today*?' If we are to go along with the basic sociological premise that all knowledge is socially situated, as articulated by the standpoint theories of Patricia Hill Collins (1986) and Sandra Harding (2004), then it makes plain sense that at a time of global empires and colonialism, many sociologists in the metropole would be reproducing the points of view formed by empires and colonialism (concerning colonial difference, the superiority of the West and so on). However, the issue is not only one of describing sociology's past. Rather, decolonizing sociology involves carefully showing how sociology developed in the context of colonialism and empire, how it both supported and reproduced colonial ways of thinking and representing the world, and how sociology *continues* to adhere to this colonial logic.

A useful way to think about the durability of sociology's colonial logic is the move from formal colonialism to coloniality more generally. Colonialism – as a formal administration, involving the 'creation of an organization controlled by members of the conquering polity and suited to rule over the conquered territory's indigenous population' (Steinmetz 2014: 79) – still carries on today (for example, in Puerto Rico, as well as settler colonies such as the US, New Zealand and Australia). However, after World War II, we saw the formal 'decolonization' of most of the world. The concept of *coloniality* is then invoked in order for us to understand how the power relationships born in colonialism *outlived the demise of colonial administrations*. As two coloniality scholars, Nelson Maldonado-Torres and Ramón Grosfoguel, thus summarize:

> Coloniality is different from colonialism. Colonialism denotes a political and economic relation in which the sovereignty of a nation or a people rests on the power

of another nation, which makes such nation an empire.
Coloniality, instead, refers to long-standing patterns
of power that emerged as a result of colonialism, but
that define culture, labor, intersubjective relations, and
knowledge production well beyond the strict limits
of colonial administrations. Thus, coloniality survives
colonialism. (Maldonado-Torres 2007: 243)

One of the most powerful myths of the twentieth
century was the notion that the elimination of colonial
administrations amounted to the decolonization of the
world. [...] Although 'colonial administrations' have
been almost entirely eradicated and the majority of
the periphery is politically organized into independent
states, non-European people are still living under crude
European/Euro-American exploitation and domination.
The old colonial hierarchies of European versus
non-Europeans remain in place and are entangled with
the 'international division of labor' and accumulation of
capital at a world-scale. (Grosfoguel 2007: 219)

With coloniality, therefore, we get the reproduction of
the relationships born in colonialism despite the fact that
'official' colonialism may not still be in place. Du Bois (1954:
1) thus describes the power relationships from colonialism to
coloniality involving a 'change in method of control [...] but
not real change in the facts or rigor of results', thus creating
a new phase of global imperialism.

Furthermore, the logic of this global imperialism of the
present day is still firmly rooted in the notion of colonial
difference. As Grosfoguel (2017: 158) therefore states on the
continuity of colonial difference, over the past five centuries,
the Western world has positioned itself as the heart of God's
earth, the centre and incarnation of civilization, the truly
'developed' world, and the leaders and warriors of world
democracy, thus justifying actions from enslavement and
colonialism through to the imposition of economic laws and
military intervention in the 'unruly', backward Global South:

During the last 520 years of the 'European/Euro-North-American capitalist/patriarchal modern/colonial world-system' we went from 'convert to Christianity or I'll kill you' in the 16th century, to 'civilize or I'll kill you' in the 18th and 19th centuries, to 'develop or I'll kill you' in the 20th century, and more recently, the 'democratize or I'll kill you' at the beginning of the 21st century.

Coloniality: Coloniality refers to how the relations put in place through colonialism outlived the collapse of colonial administrations. It thus bears a similarity to other regularly used terms such as neo-colonialism (Hall 1996) and neo-imperialism (Mandle 1967). Central to the premise of coloniality is that the relations put in place through colonialism, which continue today, are not just to do with economic relations of exploitation and expropriation, but are also *ontological* and *epistemological*.

Colonial difference: Colonial difference was a myth produced through colonialism that itself buttressed colonial rule. The myth of colonial difference was that the colonized were somehow different from (and inferior to) the 'West'. Colonial difference was the central epistemological, ontological scheme that allowed empires to construe the rest of the world as 'backward' and uncivilized, in need of colonial intervention.

It therefore becomes myopic to dismiss any talk of contemporary decolonization by simply saying something along the lines of 'colonialism was something that happened a long time ago'. Even if colonialism (in most places) did end a long time ago, the matrix of power – with its epistemic and ontological dimensions – born in colonialism continues in the present day. Further, if this matrix of power continues in the present day under the banner of coloniality, then we have little reason to assume that sociology automatically shook off its colonial logic upon the demise of empires. Instead, as per the reality of coloniality, it seems more apt to assume that sociology's commitment to the colonial episteme – or what Walter Mignolo (2002) and Patel (2014) term the 'coloniality of knowledge' – outlived formal colonial rule. It is the aim of this book to track how sociology maintains its commitment to the colonial episteme, how various thinkers within sociology have sought to challenge this, and what we can all do to work towards a more effective *decolonial* sociology. In order to fully realize these aims, it is useful to briefly clarify how a 'decolonial sociology' maintains some differences from other sociological approaches that may, at first sight, appear similar in their aims.

Decolonial sociology and ...

Throughout the following chapters I will seek to explore the varying dimensions of what characterizes 'colonial' sociology, what a contrasting decolonial sociology therefore involves, and how we can work to make sociology a decolonial enterprise (and why we should want to do this). This introductory chapter has focused on reflecting on sociology's emergent years, particularly examining how many classical sociologists worked to reproduce the colonial episteme, and in doing so, buttressed the myth of colonial difference. While 'colonial sociology' involves more than just classical sociologists reproducing colonial difference, we can use these examples to highlight some salient differences between decolonial sociology and other sociological approaches. In doing so, we can begin to start working out what decolonial sociology *is not*.

To begin with, it is worth realizing that a decolonial sociology is much more than a 'global' sociology. Simply turning one's attention away from Europe and the US to 'other' places in the Global South does not necessarily create a decolonial approach. The revisionist history of sociology provided in this chapter, for instance, shows that classical sociologists *were* global in their outlook. However, it was these very same 'global' sociologists who were reproducing colonial difference. Just because Durkheim studied indigenous people across the world, this does not mean that Durkheim was a decolonial scholar; rather, Durkheim used these studies of indigenous people to reproduce colonial ideas of savagery, civilization and societal evolution. Similarly, as we explore in the following chapter in more detail, both Marx (1973 [1939]) and Weber (1959, 2000 [1958]) compared the religions and economic structures of the 'East' with the West in order to form their analyses of European capitalism and modernity. However, again, given that both of them merely reproduced colonial ideas that non-Western societies were 'backward' and static, despite the fact that these were 'global sociologies' they were not decolonial sociologies.

By a similar logic, decolonial sociology is not the same thing as the sociology of race.[14] Of course, as I mentioned, race itself was created in and through colonialism, and provided the overall scaffolding for the notion of colonial difference. However, this does not mean that the sociology of race is necessarily a decolonial sociology. For instance, critical race theory – a key paradigm in the sociology of race – as theorized by Eduardo Bonilla-Silva (2015), revolves around the premise that contemporary racism is relatively autonomous from histories of colonialism. Another popular rival theory – Michael Omi and Howard Winant's (1994) racial formation theory – also holds that in societies such as the US, colonialism and imperialism are no longer pertinent in their racial projects. Both of these key 'race studies' paradigms, therefore, go directly against the concept of coloniality – that the world is still shaped by the colonial matrix of power. Thinking more historically, scholars such as Du Bois (1898) and Franklin Frazier (1947) have shown that most of their white contemporaries working in the sociology of race were doing so precisely to reproduce ideas of the inherent racial inferiority of Black Americans – there is certainly nothing 'decolonial' about this.[15] Indeed, in order to challenge this

uncritical sociology of race, Du Bois founded the Atlanta
Sociological Laboratory in 1896 in order to study social
problems faced by Black US Americans in inner cities (see
Wright 2002a). However, given that this work produced by
the Atlanta School from 1896 to 1924 focused solely on these
specific problems, it still was not decolonial in that it was not
interested in linking these social problems in the urban US to
wider transnational processes.[16] As critical as much sociology
of race is, and despite the fact that you can have decolonial
sociologies of race, there is no guarantee that the sociology of
race will *necessarily* be a decolonial sociology.

Of course, no one is reading this book to find out what
decolonial sociology is not. Rather, at least I hope, people are
reading this book to find out more about what is entailed by
a decolonial sociology, and why this approach is needed in
the first place. Before proceeding to this discussion, I briefly
highlight the route this book takes through colonial and
decolonial sociology.

Outline of the book

In chapter 1, 'The Decolonial Challenge to Sociology',
I seek to further specify how dominant sociology often
universalizes from a 'Western' perspective, elides connections between this 'West' and the rest, or does discuss those
in the Global South, but from a perspective that reproduces
colonial difference. I demonstrate this colonial episteme by
considering examples from the 'holy trinity' of Marx, Weber
and Durkheim, through to more contemporary sociologists
working today. I then consider what 'challenge' a decolonial
sociology launches towards this dominant way of thinking.
In particular, I pay attention to how a decolonial sociology
gives birth to a radical relationism, and seeks to both value
and recognize the agency of those in the Global South.
Through this relationism, decolonial sociology stresses interconnections between time and space which overcome the
'bifurcation' – or splitting of the world into the West and the
rest – which forms the basis of the colonial episteme.

In chapter 2, 'Beyond Intellectual Imperialism', I then turn my attention to those who have tried to radically break from sociology's dominant ways of thinking. I begin by analysing the claims that sociology is involved in an 'intellectual imperialism', whereby ideas and theories manufactured in the Global North are exported to the Global South. In critiquing this political economy of knowledge, I consider claims that this intellectual imperialism leads to a situation of mental captivity or extraversion, whereby sociologists in the South must constantly engage with Northern theories and institutions in order for their work to be valued. Against this backdrop of intellectual imperialism, this chapter then considers those who have attempted to challenge the unequal ways knowledge is produced in sociology, paying specific attention to the calls for 'indigenous' and 'autonomous' sociologies. In assessing these calls for indigenous and autonomous sociologies, this chapter considers how Eurocentrism can still seep into attempts to decolonize sociology.

In chapter 3, 'Walking While Asking Questions', I consider a decolonial approach which focuses on building sociology through horizontal conversations between different epistemological traditions. In doing so, I highlight how decolonial sociology is not about burning books, it is not about preventing all sociologists from uttering the names 'Marx, Weber, Durkheim', and it is not about labelling European thinkers as racist and/or colonial apologists. Rather, I show how decolonial sociology involves finding links between theorists and theories across the world. I demonstrate this by looking at how Du Bois, Frantz Fanon and Ali Shari'ati all engage with the works of Marx, before then considering the anti-colonial roots of both Pierre Bourdieu's and Michel Foucault's social thought, as well as the links between the coloniality of gender approach and recent articulations of intersectionality.

I then conclude in 'Sociology and the Decolonial Option'. In this chapter, I firstly consider the necessity of embracing the decolonial option for sociology to move forwards. I argue that in order to fully understand one of the key problems of our time – the climate crisis – we need to embrace a decolonial sociology. Through embracing such a decolonial sociology we can gain better understandings of the climate crisis, by rethinking our concepts of humanism, nature and agency to better locate people as part of an overall environment. I take this instance of going beyond Western sociology to argue that decolonizing sociology entails radically widening our scope of methodologies, thus reviewing indigenous sociological approaches in doing so. In this chapter, I also put forward the idea that 'decolonizing sociology' is an ongoing process with no set end or goal. Given that it is an ongoing process, I finish this chapter, and this book, with a list of thinking points and questions for us to constantly ask ourselves as we seek to embrace and practise the decolonial option in sociology. What exactly the decolonial option entails is now what we turn to.

Further reading

Articles

Connell, R. W. 1997. 'Why Is Classical Theory Classical?' *American Journal of Sociology* 102 (6): 1511–57.

Raewyn Connell examines how classical sociologists – including Émile Durkheim, Max Weber, Herbert Spencer and Lester Ward, among many more – reproduced ideas of colonial difference. Connell's paper thus resituates the development of sociology in the context of colonialism, and critiques the process through which this history of sociology has been erased from dominant understandings of the discipline.

Go, Julian. 2014. 'Beyond Metrocentrism: From Empire to Globalism in Early US Sociology'. *Journal of Classical Sociology* 14 (2): 178–202.

Julian Go examines how the first sociologists in the United States in the nineteenth and early twentieth centuries were largely concerned with the issues of colonialism, imperialism and empire. Through investigating publications such as the

American Journal of Sociology, as well through examining the courses being taught in sociology at this time, Go thus challenges the idea that sociologists in the United States were not concerned with global affairs.

Steinmetz, George. 2013. 'A Child of the Empire: British Sociology and Colonialism, 1940s–1960s'. *Journal of the History of the Behavioral Sciences* 49 (4): 353–78.

George Steinmetz's paper looks specifically at British sociology, investigating how the discipline emerged in the context of the British empire. Steinmetz points out not only that many early British sociologists played a role in colonial administrations, but that the British state saw sociology as a key discipline in generating knowledge about their colonies. Steinmetz's paper thus shows how sociology reproduced both epistemic and material components of British colonial rule.

Books

Connell, Raewyn. 2007. *Southern Theory: The Global Dynamics of Knowledge in Social Science*. Cambridge: Polity. (Part 1).

In this passage of her book, Raewyn Connell situates the development of sociology in its imperial and colonial origins. Connell pays attention to 'classical' sociology in this context of empire and colonialism, while discussing how this history of sociology continues to have epistemic consequences today.

Go, Julian. 2016. *Postcolonial Thought and Social Theory*. New York, NY: Oxford University Press. (Introduction).

Much like Connell, in this passage of his book, Julian Go examines the institutionalization of sociology in the midst of colonialism. Within this introduction, Go also compares how alongside the institutionalization of colonial sociology, we see emerging currents of anti-colonial and postcolonial thought.

–1–

The Decolonial Challenge to Sociology

While the previous chapter focused on how sociology supported and strengthened the colonial episteme of its time, this chapter turns to how this colonial episteme has influenced classical and contemporary sociology, and how decolonialism challenges this vision of sociology. Indeed, this notion of challenging a 'vision' of sociology is especially pertinent to our discussion, as it highlights the presence of differing 'standpoints' in the discipline.

While the notion of 'standpoint theory' was coined through feminist scholarship in the twentieth century, largely through the works of Patricia Hill Collins (1986) and Sandra Harding (1987), the notion of *standpoint* has been central to critical sociology since the discipline's development in the nineteenth century. One of the first critical sociologists in the US, W. E. B. Du Bois (1898), for instance, as well as his contemporaries such as Frazier (1947), made the notion of standpoint central to their critiques of US sociology. Both Du Bois (1898) and Frazier (1947) specifically focused on how white sociologists of race in the US were setting out to merely reproduce the idea of Black inferiority rather than conducting rigorous sociological research on the matter.[1] As Du Bois (1898: 13–14) thus claimed 'It is so easy for a man who has already formed his conclusions to receive any and all testimony in their favor without carefully weighing and testing it, that we sometimes find in serious scientific studies very curious proof of broad conclusions', resulting in a situation in sociology whereby 'our opinions upon the Negro are more matters of faith than of knowledge' (Du Bois 1898: 14–15).

Foundational to the concept of standpoint theory, as it developed in the tradition of Black sociology, therefore, was a critique of the 'artificial distinction between analysis and analysts' (Bonilla-Silva and Zuberi 2008: 4). Standpoint theory thus stresses how the notion of disinterested, 'objectively produced' knowledge is a myth that serves to obscure power relations. Rather than buying into the myth of the 'objective I' in sociology, as Collins (1986, 1998) highlights, standpoint theory enables us to see that knowledge produced by dominant social groups tends to reproduce their worldview(s), while knowledge produced in the academy from marginalized people produces alternative 'outsider' perspectives from within the discipline. Standpoints, therefore, are not just referring to individual researchers' individual identities and tying these identities to particular epistemological commitments. Rather, standpoint theory is a much wider systemic critique of how certain positions in the academic field – including visions of what the discipline should look like, what type of theory, methods and research 'belongs' to the discipline, what rules the discipline should abide by, and the valuation/devaluation of different knowledges within the discipline – become dominant and reproduced by certain social groups, while other standpoints remain marginalized.

The Eurocentric standpoint in sociology

It is in this spirit of thought that this chapter begins by analysing the particular standpoint of the colonial episteme in sociology. The standpoint belonging to this colonial episteme may be labelled as the standpoint of 'Northern theory' (Connell 2006)[2] or the Eurocentric standpoint (Alatas 2014).[3]

When people hear charges of Eurocentrism in sociology, they typically think that the criticism being developed is that the sociological canon tends to be dominated by European or Western thinkers. Indeed, it is true that the canon has developed this way across the world, as Syed Farid Alatas (2010: 29) highlights:

> Typically, a history of social thought or a course on social thought and theory would cover theorists such as Montesquieu, Vico, Comte, Spencer, Marx, Weber, Durkheim, Simmel, Toennies, Sombart, Mannheim, Pareto, Sumner, Ward, Small and others. Generally, non-Western thinkers are excluded.

However, the critique of Eurocentrism is not necessarily a critique of European thinkers. Rather, it is a critique of a standpoint, where sociology adopts 'a particular position, a perspective, a way of seeing *and* not-seeing that is rooted in a number of problematic claims and assumptions' (Alatas and Sinha 2001: 319). In particular, following Go (2016a), it will be argued that the Eurocentric standpoint is characterized by two principles: Orientalism and bifurcation.

Eurocentric standpoint: The Eurocentric standpoint is a particular way of looking at social reality. In particular, this viewpoint is often characterized by Orientalism, in virtue of producing ideas about the non-Western world as being backward or less civilized than the Western world. This can be seen, for instance, in Weber (1959, 2000 [1958]) and Marx (1973 [1939]) both seeing non-Western societies as static and pre-modern. The Eurocentric standpoint is also characterized by bifurcation. Through this bifurcation, the West is seen as being different from 'the rest' of the world, and it is held that you can both study the West independently from its relation to the rest, and build universal theory from studying this isolated West.

Orientalism in the Eurocentric standpoint

The concept of Orientalism was developed through postcolonial thinkers in the humanities and cultural studies, typically being associated with scholars such as Edward Saïd, Homi Bhabha, Gayatri Spivak and Stuart Hall. As Saïd (1979: 2) comments, Orientalism 'is a style of thought' emerging in the colonial era 'based upon an ontological and epistemological distinction made between "the Orient" and (most of the time) "the Occident"'. Central to the work of those theorizing Orientalism is the idea that the binaries and 'ontological and epistemological' distinctions between the West and the East (Saïd 1979), the Occident and Orient (Ahmed 2006), or simply what Hall (1992) labels the West and the rest, *are produced by the West*. Moreover, these binaries produced by the West are not value-neutral, but inherently convey a supposition of 'Eastern' or 'Oriental' difference and inferiority. Saïd (1979: 2–3), therefore, argued that particularly in France and England 'the basic distinction between East and West' was taken as the 'starting point for elaborate theories, epics, novels, social descriptions, and political accounts concerning the Orient, its people, customs, "mind", destiny, and so on'. Thus, Saïd (1979) shows how many Western canonical literary authors in the nineteenth and twentieth centuries – including Joseph Conrad, Gustave Flaubert, William Somerset Maugham, Gérard de Nerval – consistently portrayed 'the East' as a place of pre-modern, exotic, unruly life. At the same time, Saïd (1994) shows that such ideas of the East were also reproduced by famous artists such as Eugène Delacroix, George W. Joy and Henri Matisse, captured in their presentation of 'Oriental' women in hyper-sexualized ways,[4] or in their 'images of Western imperial authority' depicting European military conquests over the savage East.[5] Beyond literary and artistic practice, departments of 'Oriental studies' additionally flourished across particularly Britain and France – one of the most famous examples of this being the founding of London's School of Oriental and African Studies in 1916 – dedicated to the study of the pre-modern cultures of the Eastern world (Saïd 1979).

Theories of Orientalism, therefore, engaged with key currents in poststructuralist thought around the nature of power and categorization. Especially taking inspiration from Michel Foucault's (1990 [1976]) work, theorists of Orientalism stressed that it was the imbalance of power in colonialism which allowed for empires to effectively produce and disseminate representations of the East as being pre-modern and inferior to Western culture. Through this reading, Orientalism itself produces the category of the Orient; as Sérgio Costa (2007: 3) thus clarifies, Orientalism:

> characterizes an established and institutionalized mode of production of representations about a determined region of the world, which is nourished, confirmed, and actualized by means of the very images and knowledge that it (re-)creates.

Orientalism, therefore, can be understood as a particular discourse that itself sought to produce and crystallize colonial difference. This discourse relies on hierarchical binaries between the West and the rest, such that the sanctity of Western Christianity can be compared to the savage tribal customs of indigenous Americans and Africans, the cleanliness of Western cities can be contrasted to the squalor of the Middle East and South Asia, Western sexual respectability can be contrasted to the promiscuity and amorality of African women, and the civility of everyday life in the bourgeois West can be contrasted with the rudeness of the East.[6]

Orientalism was a central part of classical sociology, as it enabled comparisons between the West and the rest which justified the idea of Western superiority. In some cases, this sociological Orientalism was directly tied to happenings in the nation state. In the US, Edward Ross (1901: 77), for instance, clearly reproduced the US state's xenophobia towards Chinese migrants and Jewish refugees in the early twentieth century, when his critique of immigration included the argument that:

> The Jew, on the other hand, turns his face toward the future. He is thrifty and always ready for a good stroke

of business, will, indeed, join with his worst enemy if it pays. He is calculating, enterprising, migrant and ambitious. [...] It is, then, no wonder that the Jews and the Chinese are the two most formidable mercantile races in the world today.

It was this logic, endorsed by Ross among others, that created such strong support for Chinese exclusion acts and rejection of asylum for Jewish refugees in the early twentieth century in the US. In terms of Orientalism outside of the US, we can focus on Marx and Weber.

Both Marx and Weber were attempting to explain the Western transition into industrial capitalism, or what we can also label broadly as 'modernity'. However, in order to explain this Western transition into capitalism, both Marx and Weber have an Orientalism at the core of their theories. For instance, Marx (1973 [1939], 2004 [1867]) argued that Western societies transitioned from feudalism into capitalism as there was a shift in the means of production (which were becoming increasingly industrial), and an unequal ownership of these means of production, which created the driving force of class antagonism between the workers and bourgeoisie. To Marx, this tension between the two classes was then the spirit of capitalism, as the workers earn just enough for subsistence, while the bourgeoisie extract the surplus capital from the workers' labour. This class struggle as a driving force for development in the West is contrasted to what Marx (1973 [1939]) labels as the 'Asiatic mode of production' that we see in the so-called East ('Asiatic societies'). In such a mode of production, Marx argues, the society is in stagnation due to the absence of a dynamic class struggle, and to a state-centralized economy with no private ownership of land.[7]

Parallel to Marx, we have Weber (2001 [1905]) arguing that central to the Western development of capitalism is a 'Protestant ethic', characterized by an asceticism which rejects the search for everyday pleasures and instead fosters a stringent dedication to work. Along with this ascetic will to work, Weber argues that the growth of European cities and increased specialization of the workforce led to the industrialization of the West as we know it. Just like Marx, Weber compares this situation in the West with what he saw as stagnant societies in the East – the Chinese, Indian and Muslim 'worlds' – which were seen to have religions of 'sensuality' that did not have the discipline required for industrial work.[8] Weber (2001 [1905]: xxviii) even goes as far as to deny the presence of critical or 'scientific' thought in these apparently stagnant societies, as is captured in the introduction to his *The Protestant Ethic and the Spirit of Capitalism*:

> A product of modern European civilization, studying any problem of universal history, is bound to ask himself to what combination of circumstances the fact should be attributed that in Western civilization, and in Western civilization only, cultural phenomena have appeared which (as we like to think) lie in a line of development having *universal* significance and value. Only in the West does science exist at a stage of development which we recognize to-day as valid.

Of course, Weber's argument for the lack of scientific thought outside the West is spurious. Speaking specifically about Islam, for instance, Ali Shari'ati (1986: 44) hits the nail on the head when he makes reference to the fact that the Moors conquered, and economically, intellectually and socially advanced, large areas of Spain up until the fifteenth century; as Shari'ati states, 'prior to reaching the threshold of universal colonization and economic imperialism, the West knew Islam very well. Islam has built one of the greatest civilizations of the world in Europe itself, in Spain.' As captured in Shari'ati's insight, Weber's dismissal of non-Western thought relies on quite significant historical inaccuracies. Indeed, once we start analysing the claims that Marx and Weber make about the 'non-Western world', we can see that historical inaccuracy is fairly typical. Further, it is through these historical inaccuracies that Marx and Weber are able to contribute to the notion of difference between the West and the rest through the discourse of Orientalism.

Thus, as summarized by Bryan Turner (1989), one of the central critiques of Marx and Weber is that neither of them gathered sufficient research material to make their sweeping generalizations about 'Asiatic societies', with Weber in particular deliberately ignoring the work of his contemporary Sinologists.

The historiography that Marx and Weber overlooked presented quite a different argument from what was put forward in their seminal theories. In terms of China, for instance, Enrique Dussel (2002) shows that prior to colonialism the Chinese were the leaders of the global political economy, partly through their richness in gold and silver, the two most valuable trading materials. Similarly, as shown by Bhambra (2007), prior to colonialism, India was the leading exporter of valuable materials such as cotton and textiles. In both the Chinese and Indian cases, their richness in the textile industry, as well as their richness in terms of resources such as gold and silver, came not from a nationalized economy, but rather from a specialization of labour that Weber and Marx both see as typical only of the Western economies; in fact, as Bhambra (2007) points out, India actually practised the specialization of labour in the cotton-weaving industry before the British mimicked this strategy and imported it into the British textile industry.

Through their historical inaccuracies, Marx and Weber also overlook the work of people whose research focus was explicitly on the dynamic nature of 'Asiatic societies'. Ibn Khaldūn, for instance, was already analysing such dynamism of 'Asian societies' long before Marx and Weber came to generalize across this whole region.

Writing in the fourteenth century, Ibn Khaldūn (2015 [1370]) focused on how nomadic societies developed into sedentary societies, invoking the concept of *asabiyya*, which can be understood as group solidarity. Khaldūn's (2015 [1370]) argument was that in nomadic society, or a society characterized by rival groups, eventually the group with the strongest asabiyya conquers the others and we get the formation of a sedentary society as one group rules. Just as with Marx's later theory of internal contradiction being a driver of societal change, Khaldūn (2015 [1370]) argues that within this sedentary society, new nomadic groups come into society and the asabiyya of the dominant group begins to fracture, and we then get an increase in rival tension leading us back into a nomadic society. To Khaldūn, therefore, societies were not stagnant but constantly moving circularly from nomadic into sedentary societies, back to nomadic and then sedentary societies, and so on. Thus, Khaldūn was already stressing the dynamic nature of those societies which Marx and Weber would later gloss over as stagnant. Furthermore, inside this Khaldūnian paradigm, we also have a tradition that can help us to analyse other societies across the Asian continent in a way that escapes the Orientalism of Marx and Weber's theories. Syed Farid Alatas (1993), for instance, uses Khaldūn's theory of societal development to analyse the Safavi economy in sixteenth- and seventeenth-century Iran. In this case, Alatas argues that the Safavi economy was not merely one of complete state control as implied by the Marxist 'Asiatic mode of production'. In contrast, this economy was characterized by a range of interme-diaries between the state and peasantry who served a similar economic function to the bourgeoisie in Marxist and Weberian theories of capitalism – whether that be former peasants who had taken part in the military and been rewarded with land on which they could charge tax, or the *ulama* (religious clerics) who could collect tax on land and surplus value from labour.

Inside the theories of Marx and Weber, therefore, we can see 'their arguments in terms of broad, simple, contrasting oppositions which mirror quite closely the West–Rest, civilized–rude, developed–backward oppositions of "the

West and the Rest" discourse' (Hall 1992: 223). Through crystallizing this West/rest binary, furthermore, Weber and Marx consequently offered internalist accounts of capitalism and modernity that made it appear as though capitalism developed in the West because of particular conditions *within* the West (the class structure, the Protestant ethic), while it did not develop in the rest of the world because of factors internal to those parts of the world (Hinduism, Islam, Confucianism, the 'Asiatic mode of production'). Through these internalist accounts of capitalism and modernity, however, we see how Marx and Weber occlude analysis of the connections between the West and the rest in the development of capitalism. We lose sight of the fact that, as Fanon (1963 [1961]: 102) put it, the West is 'literally the creation of the Third World', as the 'third world' – in the form of colonies or imperial territories – provided the labour, land and natural resources for the overdevelopment of Western economies. Weber may have labelled China as a stagnant society, but he did not note how the Spanish colonization of the Americas enabled them to steal enough silver and gold to make the Chinese economy plummet (Dussel 2002); Marx may have labelled India as stagnant and in need of an economic revolution, but as we have seen, over £9 billion worth of capital was channelled from India into the British economy between 1765 and 1938 (Patnaik 2017). Through missing these connections between the West and the rest, Marx and Weber's Orientalism leads them to commit the second principle of the Eurocentric standpoint: bifurcation.

Bifurcation in the Eurocentric standpoint

Bifurcation in the Eurocentric standpoint is characterized by the belief that one can separate the West from the rest of the world, and analyse the West outside of its global links (Bhambra 2007; Go 2016a). We encountered this form of bifurcation when discussing Marx and Weber, and how both of these thinkers largely analysed the rise of Western capitalism as separate from Western states' colonial projects and capital-accumulating/expropriating colonial regimes. In the cases of Marx and Weber, it was not simply an issue of them dismissing the existence of a Global South – as we discussed, they both wrote on India, China and the so-called 'Muslim world' – but rather an issue of not making links between what was happening in the West and what these same Western countries were doing in these apparently stagnant regions. This leads to confusing situations where, for instance, in volume 3 of *Capital*, Marx (1998 [1894]) becomes able to talk about the importance of European countries' wealth in 'precious metals' for their capital development and trade, without mentioning that such materials were expropriated from colonial territories and imported into the metropoles.

Furthermore, we can see this form of bifurcation beyond these 'classical' sociologists of the nineteenth century, even in paradigms of social thought that were positioned as being highly critical, such as – as the name suggests – critical theory. Within this paradigm of critical theory, perhaps one of the more obvious examples of bifurcation appears in the works of Jürgen Habermas, who fails to think about how European empires' colonial authoritarianism allowed for the emergence of bourgeois liberal culture in the West. In his (2015 [1962]) *The Structural Transformation of the Public Sphere*, for instance, Habermas analyses how in nineteenth-century Western Europe, the emergence of institutions such as coffee houses extended the public sphere to include larger numbers of the cultural bourgeoisie in the civic apparatus of the nation state. Of course, as Go (2016a) points out, coffee itself was a colonial product, and not a product that was willingly 'traded' by colonial territories but a resource that was forcibly expropriated.[9] In this case, therefore, authoritarian control in one part of the world facilitated the rise of a bourgeois liberal culture in the other.

Indeed, we can stay with critical theory to look at a slightly more complex example of bifurcation. Max Horkheimer and Theodor Adorno (2002 [1944]), for instance, extensively focused on what they termed the 'dialectic of Enlightenment', the process through which the European Enlightenment's valorization of rationalism and

scientific inquiry collapsed into the scientific fascism epito-
mized by Nazi Germany. However, in isolating the horrors
of Nazism as *the* epitome of the dialectic of Enlightenment
and modernity, the position adopted by Adorno and
Horkheimer fails to connect the horrors of Nazi Germany
with the long history of violence towards colonized people
across the various empires, *which itself acted as a precursor
to Nazism.*[10] As Patrick Wolfe (2006) has shown, many of
the tactics deployed by Nazis in the Holocaust, for instance,
were based on models of genocide used in the Spanish
colonization of the Americas (such as the random shooting
sprees in concentration camps), and the British colonization
of Ireland and Bengal (such as starvation to death); indeed,
as Clarence Lusane (2004) highlights, the first recorded
genocide of the twentieth century – the Herero and Nama
genocide in present-day Namibia – was not only executed
by the German empire, but was led by figures such as Eugen
Fischer, later involved in organizing the apparatus of the
Holocaust. As Aimé Césaire (2001 [1950]: 36) thus shows
in his *Discourse on Colonialism*, seeing Nazism and the
practices of empires as bifurcated clouds our ability to see
the true logic of terror imbued in modernity:

> Yes, it would be worthwhile to study clinically, in detail,
> the steps taken by Hitler and Hitlerism and to reveal to
> the very distinguished, very humanistic, very Christian
> bourgeois of the twentieth century that without his
> being aware of it, he has a Hitler inside him, that
> Hitler inhabits him, that Hitler is his demon, that if he
> rails against him, he is being inconsistent and that, at
> bottom, what he cannot forgive Hitler for is not crime
> in itself, the crime against man, it is not the humili-
> ation of man as such, it is the crime against the white
> man, the humiliation of the white man, and the fact
> that he applied to Europe colonialist procedures which
> until then had been reserved exclusively for the Arabs
> of Algeria, the coolies of India, and the [redacted][11] of
> Africa.

However, bifurcation does not just separate out the links between the West and the rest. As summarized by Meghan Tinsley (2019), bifurcation in sociology also involves the drawing of an epistemic line between the West and the rest, and accepting the idea that if one's theoretical model works on 'this side' of the line – on the Western side – then it can achieve universality. It is this form of bifurcation in sociology that has led to charges of what Bhambra (2014) terms 'methodological Eurocentrism', and why Dipesh Chakrabarty (2009a) calls for the need to 'provincialize' European social thought. Central to understanding this epistemic bifurcation is that it is not necessarily an explicit strategy adopted by particular sociologists – it is not the case that sociologists have consciously signed a document agreeing that if their theories work in the West, they work everywhere. Rather, this epistemic bifurcation is built into the 'disciplinary unconscious' of sociology; it is an essential feature of most sociology regardless of whether or not the sociologists guilty of this bifurcation are cognizant of their actions. This unconscious working of epistemic bifurcation is well captured in Connell's (2018: 401) quote that:

> In mainstream theory (including methodology), there is little sense of being the product of such a specific milieu. Read a modern classic text like Garfinkel's *Studies in Ethnomethodology*, Coleman's *Foundations of Social Theory*, Bourdieu's *Logic of Practice*, or Habermas's *Theory of Communicative Action* and you will see, rather, an assumption that the thoughts produced here simply apply universally.[12]

It is precisely because of the fact that it is buried in the disciplinary unconscious that epistemic bifurcation is so powerful; it allows for copious seminal theories to be presented as universal in a way that denies any sense of the agency, reality or existence of those in the South. Foucault, for instance, is taken to be not just a seminal social theorist, but a seminal figure in the arts, humanities and social sciences more broadly. However, the theory of disciplinary power that Foucault (2019 [1975]) offers is guilty of precisely this epistemic bifurcation that we have been discussing. Namely, Foucault (2019 [1975]) argues that in Western Europe, around the time of the eighteenth century, there is a shift in the exercise of power, where criminals ceased to be punished through the 'spectacle of scaffold' (i.e. public execution and/or torture), and instead are hidden away in prisons. Foucault's argument is that this model of power in the prison can be generalized to understanding disciplinary power in society, where citizens are regulated through surveillance and a normalizing gaze. The issue with Foucault's account of disciplinary power is not *just* that it only focuses on Western Europe; had Foucault linked the 'covert' surveillance-style power in the metropoles with the overtly violent exercise of power in the colonies, then this would indeed be a critical argument. The issue with Foucault's viewpoint is that he offers no justification for why he *only* focuses on Western Europe for modelling this theory of power – it is here we see the assumed universality of the West which is buried in the disciplinary unconscious.

Further, this disciplinary unconscious thus leads us to a Eurocentric standpoint which offers, at best, a thoroughly obfuscated vision of social realities. As Connell (2006: 261) puts to Foucault:

One hundred years after the execution of Damiens the regicide, when Foucault's 'reticence' was supposedly in full flow, the British executed a large number of men they captured while suppressing the 'Indian Mutiny' in 1857–58. They did it in public, with exemplary brutality, including mass hangings and floggings, caste degradation of leaders, and blowing rebels from the cannon's mouth. Public, spectacular, collective punishments remained a favored technique of British and French colonialism far into the twentieth century. Notable examples are the punitive massacres at Setif and Kerrata in 1945, to intimidate the populations of northern Africa, just after France itself had been liberated from the Nazis.

The bifurcation in Foucault's account of disciplinary power, therefore, fails to provide a convincing account of social reality given that 'his theory arbitrarily cuts "Europe" off from its colonies – as if imperial and colonial history were not also Europe's history' (Go 2016a: 89). Furthermore, we can see this form of epistemic bifurcation even in sociological paradigms which have deliberately sought to be 'global' in their outlook.

As Connell (2007b) points out in 'The Northern Theory of Globalization', sociologists writing from the 1990s onwards dedicated a lot of energy to the issue of globalization. However, rather than seeing it as an economic programme, these sociologists saw globalization as a *type of society* (Connell 2007b). The way that these sociologists of globalization – such as Ulrich Beck (1992, 2000) and Anthony Giddens (1990, 2002) – theorized this society, however, consistently erased the interlinkages between the West and the rest that were formed through empires, enslavement and colonialism. Thus, Beck (1992: 2) states how globalized society involves 'a new kind of global order, a new kind of society and a new kind of personal life [...] coming into being, all of which differ from earlier phases of social development'. Giddens (2002) shares with Beck the idea that globalized society involves a process of new global interconnections that have rapidly shrunk the time–space continuum across the world. Built into these understandings of global society as a 'new society', therefore, is a standpoint that overlooks how we have lived in globally interconnected societies since the formation of colonialism. For instance, as highlighted by Eric Williams (1944), in the eighteenth and nineteenth centuries, popular consumer goods in the West, such as tea, coffee, chocolate and silk, were not produced internally by the nation state but rather came from expropriating resources from their vast colonial networks. The suggestions that globalized societies were 'new' in the way that they featured a novel global capitalist society thus seem to rely on a bifurcation that overlooks the 'age of (modern) empires'.

Further, as Connell (2007b) and Bhambra (2007) show, through this elision of Southern realities and presentation of globalization as 'new', such sociologists only present a partial view of global interconnectedness. Specifically, such theories of globalization end up viewing it in terms of its impact on Western societies – despite the fact that such theories claim themselves to have a global focus. As Connell (2007b) shows, this results in theorists such as Giddens (2002) and Beck (1992) discussing globalization in terms of the greater presence of 'risk' (social and financial) in Western states, the possibilities of Western financial crises, and the coming need to deal with multicultural 'difference' in (supposedly) previously mostly homogeneous Western nations. What happens in such a case is that 'sociological theorizing about globalization embeds a view of the world from the global North' (Connell 2007b: 378). This does not mean that theories of globalization are 'wrong', but simply that they cannot be taken as universal.

What is being stressed in the critique of bifurcation, therefore, is not necessarily a charge of falsity or empirical incorrectness, but rather one of *incompleteness*. For instance, consider looking at a building straight on with your right eye closed. Your left eye can still see a large proportion of the building. You can observe plenty of details, such as the colour of the building, its height and so on. However, because your right eye is closed you still do not have an idea of the total picture of the building, you do not know whether what you have observed on one side of the building is generalizable to the whole building (e.g. is the building multicoloured?), and you cannot see how the visible portions of building are necessarily connected to the portions you cannot see in virtue of closing one eye. This is a summary, albeit rather a simplistic one, of how bifurcation forms part of an overall Eurocentric *standpoint*. Eurocentricity is a particular way of looking at 'the building' – whether the building is modernity, the climate crisis, disciplinary power, globalization and so on. Foucault (2019 [1975]) can tell us a lot about the details of power and punishment in Western Europe, but with one eye closed he cannot give us a more complete picture of how this 'Western' exercise of power in their metropoles connected with their brutal use of power in their colonies. Beck (1992) and Giddens (2002) can provide us with information about the rise of risk and multiculturalism in Western states, but their work looks at the building from a particular standpoint that prevents any possibility of a 'universal' theory of globalization.

At this moment it is perhaps apt to point out that in virtue of being a particular standpoint, the Eurocentric viewpoint is only one of many different standpoints within sociology. The problem is that many sociological systems which unreflexively reproduce the Eurocentric standpoint are presented as *the* universal sociology, the sociology that everyone else must equate to or position themselves towards. It is in this spirit of thought that decolonial thinkers have sought to decentre the Eurocentric standpoint, and to highlight how it is a particular strain of sociology rather than being *the* sociology itself. As Bhambra (2007: 43) comments, this decolonial approach thus encourages us to 'provincialize Europe [...] that is, to de-centre Europe in our [sociological] considerations'. In order to decentre this Eurocentric standpoint, it thus becomes necessary to engage with alternative standpoints and sociological paradigms of thought: what may be called the Southern standpoint.

Interrogating the Southern standpoint

Scholars such as Connell (2007a) have criticized the Eurocentric standpoint for producing *Northern theory*, and have contrasted that with the Southern standpoint which produces *Southern theory*. Immediately other scholars joined the conversation by problematizing the notion of Southern theory, or a Southern standpoint; after all, why should we categorize social thinkers solely through the shared connection that they are writing from a geopolitical region that was formerly colonized? As Saïd Amir Arjomand (2008: 546; see also Reed 2013) argues, does not binding disparate sets of people together solely because they are not in the West merely lead to the 'uncritical imposition of the metropolitan conceptual straightjacket [*sic*]'?

However, this criticism of essentializing a Southern stand-point opens up the very area needed to theorize a Southern standpoint in the first place. Namely, why is a shared history of colonialism *not* enough of a binding factor to constitute some broad standpoint? Decolonial thinkers from across the world have always emphasized some kind of connection between this globally colonized group as a group *for itself*, a group that recognizes its interconnectivity and recognizes that this interconnectivity will be essential for any anti-colonial practice.[13] Fanon (1963 [1961]) referred to this group as the 'wretched of the Earth'; Gayatri Spivak (2010 [1985]) similarly referred to the most destitute members of colonial society as the subaltern; South Korean intel-lectuals used the notion of a global *minjung* – translating into 'multitude of people' – to describe how anti-capitalism requires a social movement formed of excluded people from across the colonized world (Lee 2007);[14] the Jewish intel-lectual Emmanuel Levinas used the concept of 'the brave ones' as being constituted by 'third world' people who strive against the colonial matrix of power (Slabodsky 2009);[15] and Mignolo (2002) and Gloria Anzaldúa (1987) both argue that anti-colonial thought comes from the 'borders' of society – from people who live in, and think from, the margins of the colonial world system. It is not a coinci-dence that so many decolonial thinkers, writing in different times, in different geographical locations and from different religious or non-religious standpoints, have come to a similar conclusion: that the 'previously colonized' all share some sense of collective and connected histories and presents. It is from the fragments of these shared, collective and connected histories and presents that we can piece together a Southern standpoint.

In one sense, the epistemic principles of the Southern standpoint are in direct opposition to those of the Eurocentric standpoint, thus propagating a radical relationism and a rejection of Orientalism in favour of recognizing the agency of peoples across the South. However, the starting point for the Southern standpoint begins with a recognition of modernity/coloniality.

Southern standpoint: The Southern standpoint is opposed to the Eurocentric viewpoint. Through the Southern standpoint, there is an emphasis on rejecting Orientalism in favour of recognizing and valuing the agency of people and knowledges from the Global South. This recognition and valuation of the South allow for scholars like Syed Farid Alatas (1993, 2014) to draw on thinkers such as Ibn Khaldūn, and counter Orientalist depictions of Eastern societies as being static and uncivilized. The Southern standpoint is also characterized by a relationism that overcomes Eurocentric bifurcation. Thus, sociologists working from the Southern standpoint often tie processes of Western capitalism and modernity to the processes of colonial and imperial exploitation and expropriation. This is the basic premise of the concept of 'modernity/coloniality' pioneered by Walter Mignolo (2012) – the idea that modernity happened in the West *not* because of Western internalist exceptionalism, but because of the West's external (colonial) relations with the rest of the world built through their empires.

Modernity/coloniality and the formation of the Southern standpoint: relationality and recognition

Firstly, the Southern standpoint must not be thought of in terms of a geographical or ethnoracial essentialism. It is not the case that the Southern standpoint simply comes from 'Southern' countries, or from people who are racialized as not-white. As we discussed in highlighting multiple places that share histories of colonialism and imperialism, the Southern standpoint is more concerned with an *epistemic location* within the field of coloniality. This dynamic is well captured in Go's (2016b: 21) notion of *perspectival realism*, where a standpoint is understood as a 'perspective or starting point for crafting maps of the social world'. Through this theory, Go (2016b: 21) defines the Southern standpoint as follows:

> The Southern standpoint instead refers to a relational position within global hierarchies. This is a geopolitical and social position, constituted historically within broader relations of power, that embeds the viewpoint of peripheral groups. Just as feminist standpoint theory posits a standpoint defined by gendered structures, a Southern standpoint approach posits global hierarchies forged from imperial relations – past and present – as the defining relation. [...] A Southern standpoint refers not to an essence but a differential position: a position that is different from the imperial-metropolitan position of extant conventional social theory, and the difference does not lie in biological, anthropological or spatial factors but in social experience and history. What constitutes a subaltern standpoint is its positionality: it refers to the subjectivity of subordinated positions within global imperial hierarchies. It refers to a subjectivity attendant with the experience of geopolitical and global socioeconomic subjugation.

Through Go's definition, therefore, the very notion of a Southern standpoint requires us to recognize the existence of 'global hierarchies forged from imperial relations – past and present'. This does not necessarily entail that we provide some theory of globalization, but rather this involves a recognition of how colonialism, empires and imperialism brought such a degree of global interconnectedness that the whole world was brought into one particular *global field*[16] or *world system*.[17] This is not an exaggeration of the reach of colonialism and empires, given that by the time of World War I, colonial powers occupied 90 per cent of the entire land surface of the globe (Go 2016a).This relation of global interconnectedness, born through the practice of empires, colonialism and imperialism, has been labelled as the colonial/modern world system (Escobar 2007), thus relating to the concept of *modernity/ coloniality* (Mignolo 2007; Wynter 2003).

Modernity/coloniality is a concept that highlights how the overdevelopment of 'the West' (through capitalism and European modernity) happened through the underdevelopment of the rest (through colonialism, imperialism and enslavement). Already built into the concept of modernity/coloniality is therefore a *linking* between the West and the rest, thus rejecting the bifurcation popular in dominant accounts of European modernity – as we have seen with Weber and Marx in this chapter. Through starting from a recognition of modernity/coloniality, the epistemic position of the Southern standpoint is thus a counter-narrative of modernity which provides us with new theories for thinking about the world and social reality. In this regard, the concept of modernity/coloniality serves as the foundation for building the Southern standpoint within sociology.

Perhaps by now you are wondering why the concept is 'modernity/coloniality' rather than something along the lines of 'modernity and coloniality';[18] in other words, why the slash? By connecting the terms 'modernity' and 'coloniality' in one concept we are able to show their co-articulations, meaning that 'the "/" unite[s] and separate[s] them at the same time. [...] Each key word or concept is divided while at the same time connected to the [other] one' (Mignolo and Walsh 2018: 109). Through the concept of modernity/coloniality, we build a relation between two processes that we typically see as bifurcated (the rise of capitalism in the West and colonialism 'abroad'), consequently building epistemic, economic and ontological links between different parts of the world we also typically see as bifurcated (North/South, East/West etc.). It is through this approach of modernity/coloniality that decolonial scholars, therefore, have shown that without colonialism, enslavement and global empires, modernity in the West – as we know it – would not have taken shape. As Fanon (1963 [1961]: 102; emphasis added) famously put it:

From all these continents, under whose eyes Europe today raises up her tower of opulence, there has flowed out for centuries toward that same Europe diamonds and oil, silk and cotton, wood and exotic products. *Europe is literally the creation of the Third World. The wealth which smothers her is that which was stolen from the underdeveloped peoples.*

Building these relations through modernity/coloniality, we are therefore required to produce different accounts of modernity from those typically offered in canonical sociology by the likes of Marx, Durkheim, Weber and so on. Doing so enables us to highlight what scholars refer to as the 'darker side of modernity' (Mignolo 2007; Mignolo and Walsh 2018). The Southern standpoint's focus on this darker side of modernity consequently enables us to see, for instance, that it was the expropriation of materials such as gold and silver from Latin America that allowed Spain to become an economic global superpower in the sixteenth and seventeenth centuries (Quijano and Wallerstein 1992); that it was the free 'labour' of enslaved people across the world (where the enslaved simultaneously became converted into labour *and* capital) that formed the bedrock of economic development in the West (Du Bois 2014 [1935]; Williams 1944); and that it was the series of social contracts, such as the 1884–5 Berlin Conference or the nineteenth-century Doctrine of Discovery, that gave the West legal entitlement to vast amounts of capital through redistributing Africa's people, labour and natural resources (Mills 1997).

Modernity/coloniality and relational sociology

The Southern standpoint's modernity/coloniality approach, therefore, forces us into a *radical relationism*. This relational standpoint has both epistemological and ontological commitments. Ontologically, the relationism of the Southern standpoint implies that the existence of certain phenomena relies on their 'constitutive connections' with other phenomena (Go 2016a: 118). Thus, when we talk about a Global North and South, or of the metropoles and periphery (or peripheries), when we talk about men and women, Black and white, settlers and indigenous people, and so on, we are not talking about ontologically disparate binaries, but rather about constructed states of being that are necessarily connected to one another; as Pierre Bourdieu (1998: 3) puts it, 'The Real is Relational.' However, the relationism of the Southern standpoint is concerned not only with ontology and the relational co-existence of 'things', but also with *epistemology*. In particular, the Southern standpoint attempts to produce knowledge about the relations between seemingly bifurcated processes – as captured in the previous examples, which, for instance, showed the interconnections between modernity and colonialism. Relationism, therefore, becomes both an ontological mission to link categories of *social existence*, and an epistemological mission to produce knowledge of the interconnections between *social processes*. An example of this form of relationism can be seen in the work of Stuart Hall, who came to Britain from Jamaica in the 1950s.

Stuart Hall is perhaps best known for his studies of race, class and political discourse in Britain.[19] However, the way that Hall studies these issues was always from the perspective of the radical relationism which we have described as being essential to the Southern standpoint. Consider Hall's (1991: 48–9) following quote on English identity:

I am the sugar at the bottom of the English cup of tea. I am the sweet tooth, the sugar plantations that rotted generations of English children's teeth. There are thousands of others beside me that are, you know, the cup of tea itself. Because they don't grow it in Lancashire, you know. Not a single tea plantation exists within the United Kingdom. This is the symbolization of English identity – I mean, what does anybody in the world know about an English person except that they can't get through the day without a cup of tea? Where does it come from? Ceylon – Sri Lanka, India. That is the outside history that is inside the history of the English. There is no English history without that other history.

The relationism in Hall's analysis is patent. English identity is not analysed as an essential 'thing', but is shown to be relationally produced through its connections with colonialism and empire. One way Hall (1991) shows this is through focusing on the 'symbolization of English identity' – tea – as a phenomenon and social practice that is integral to English identity despite itself being imported from the colonies. Furthermore, part of the reason I have selected this quote from Hall is because it demonstrates how the relationism of the Southern standpoint is useful for pointing out not just links between things that were thought to be disparate (e.g. English identity and practices of empire), but that through building such connections we are able to *produce new knowledge of other social processes*. Thus, Hall's analysis does not just build a relation between English identity and the practices of the British empire, but also provides avenues for new understandings of phenomena, such as British nationalism.

While Hall's analysis shows us how 'there is no English history without that other history', he also provides for us a pathway into analysing how British nationalism often involves a distorted version of that 'other history'. In particular, as sociologists engaging with Hall, including Sivamohan Valluvan (2019) and Paul Gilroy (2004) have argued, such nationalism often reframes the British empire as a historical object of *pride* and *nostalgia*. In this case, therefore, Hall's relational analysis allows us to adopt the decolonial viewpoint and see how the British empire's past actions of expropriation fundamentally shaped what it means to be British in the present, while simultaneously allowing us to study how British nationalism distorts such a history in order to articulate British identity.

A relational approach is thus central to the Southern standpoint, as it encourages us to connect processes and phenomena in a way that increases our critical perspective towards the social world. Stuart Hall's work, for instance, enables us to adopt more critical perspectives towards the processes of memory formation and nationalism through a relational sociology which links English identity with coloniality.

From relationality to recognition of agency

Nevertheless, there is another key dimension to the Southern standpoint that is also realized in this quote from Hall: a recognition and valuation of Southern subjectivities. In the dominant sociological narratives of Western modernity, as Bhambra (2007) argues, the 'darker side' – of colonialism, enslavement, empires and imperialism – tends to be either invisiblized, praised or reduced to a secondary role. On the other hand, decolonial sociologists put this 'dark side' at the centre of understandings of the making of the world system. In Hall's (1991) quote we see exactly the same decolonial ethos: that despite a racially exclusive British nationalism, people from the South have fundamentally shaped what it means to be British.

Any attempts at creating a decolonial sociology, therefore, must begin from a point of recognizing and valuing the subjectivities of those from the Global South. This does not mean that a decolonial sociology simply involves incorporating Southern scholars into canons and reading lists, and nor does it mean that we start using happenings in the Global South to illustrate certain theories. Rather, as per the standpoint theory that we have been highlighting throughout this chapter, it refers to the process of developing knowledge from the borders, or frontiers, of the world system (Anzaldúa 1987), such that the knowledge systems that can speak back against the colonial matrix of power are able to be recognized, valued and developed. Indeed, decolonial scholars have pointed out that the modernity/coloniality approach itself developed from such borders of the world system

– through the writings of countless intellectuals who put
the subjectivities of Southern people at the centre of their
accounts of modernity, whether that be W. E. B. Du Bois
(2007 [1947], 2014 [1935]), Oliver Cox (1959), Fanon
(1963 [1961]), Amílcar Cabral (1966), Aimé Césaire (2001
[1950]) and so on.[20] As Mignolo and Walsh (2018: 112) thus
highlight, modernity/coloniality

> is not a concept that emerged in Europe to account
> for issues of European concern – its economy, sensi-
> bility, and history – but a concept created in the
> Third World, responding to needs prompted by local
> histories of coloniality at the very historical moment
> when the world division was collapsing. In Europe
> the concerns were on modernity, postmodernity, and
> globalization, not on coloniality, the darker side of
> modernity, postmodernity, and globalization.

In recognizing the subjectivities of people in the Global
South, and valuing these subjectivities and histories, therefore,
we are not espousing any identity essentialism but we are
making a point about the interrelation between subjugation,
resistance, epistemology and epistemic liberation. As Du Bois
(2007 [1903]) captures in his concept of double consciousness,
the subjugated acquire the gift of 'second sight'; in virtue of
their subjugation they develop critical viewpoints towards
how the world works in ways that escape the attention of the
socially dominant.[21] This is one of the many reasons why, if
sociology wishes to be critical, it must put the Southern standpoint at the centre of the discipline. Putting this Southern
standpoint at the centre of the discipline necessitates putting
the subjectivities and knowledge systems of those in the
Global South in such a central location. Looking at the state
of the sociological field, we can summarize two successful
examples of decolonial scholars putting such recognition of
Southern subjectivities at the heart of the discipline in ways
that deepen the overall analytical apparatus of sociology:
through historical sociology and through ethnography.

One way that decolonial sociology has recognized and valued the subjectivities of people in the South is through revising histories (and consequently narratives) of modernity and the making of the world system. In particular, decolonial sociology has put the Haitian revolution of 1791–1804 at the centre of our narratives and analyses of the modern world.[22] As Bhambra (2007: 149) highlights, such decolonial work not only highlights the importance of events such as the Haitian revolution to modernity, but also shows how 'the silence that surrounds the Haitian Revolution (and like events) is constitutive of the very idea of modernity and its use in sociological interpretations of the contemporary world'. As Bhambra thus argues, the Eurocentric account of modernity not only omits Southern agency, but uses this omission to justify the idea of modernity as an outcome of Western exceptionalism. Focusing on the Haitian revolution can displace this Eurocentric standpoint.

Firstly, the Haitian revolution was a moment when the claims of modernity and Enlightenment – namely, a conception of universal humanity – were (at least partially) acknowledged and constituted. Through the French Declaration of the Rights of Man (1789), a key exemplar of French revolutionary thought and practice, the French National Assembly held that 'Men are born and remain free and equal in rights' (Article I) and that 'These rights are liberty, property, safety and resistance against oppression' (Article II). Of course, at this very same time in 1789, France was not only violently controlling colonies across the world, but even in 1790 put through a series of laws that prohibited *gens de couleur* (freed Black people previously enslaved) from full citizenship (Getachew 2016). The laws and liberties that the French National Assembly thus put forward through their revolution were written as if they were universal (for instance, by using seemingly universal rather than particular terms such as 'Men', 'Man', 'Liberty' and so on), but in fact only referred to those who met the colonial criteria of full humanity. It was in this context that the Haitian revolution, as Adom Getachew (2016: 824) describes, 'forced a confrontation' between the supposed universalism of French revolutionary thought and the nation's 'practice of colonial slavery'.

The Haitian revolution, therefore, developed a concept of humanity and rights that went beyond the racialized parochialism of French revolutionary thought. Through the revolts of the enslaved against French colonial rule, starting in Saint-Domingue in 1791, we see the French republic essentially *revise* their understanding of humanity, rights, citizenship and liberty in a way that – at least in theory – continues in understandings of French republicanism today.[23] Firstly, while the revolts were proceeding, the French republic passed a series of laws allowing for 'equality of political rights' to colonized and freed men, allowing such people to now vote in local elections and run for political office (Dubois 2004, 2012). Secondly, by 1794, after a deputation from Saint-Domingue successfully argued the case to the French Constituent Assembly, France abolished the practice of enslavement (Bhambra 2007; Dubois 2004). It was thus through the actions of the enslaved and colonized that we got a new conception of humanity – a conception that spoke back against the bifurcated hierarchy of colonized and colonizer, white and Black. This requires us, therefore, to revise the Eurocentric standpoint that centres the French revolution as the triumph of reason and universal concepts of freedom and liberty – as we see, for instance, in the works of Marx (1988) and Foucault (2019 [1975]), or the critical theory school of Horkheimer and Adorno (2002 [1944]) and Habermas (2015 [1962]). As Getachew (2016: 830) thus puts it, 'the truncated ideals of the French Revolution' which were so central to the modern (and future) world were in fact realized 'by the revolutionary practices of enslaved and colonial subjects'.

Moreover, as decolonial thinkers have pointed out, lots of the historical moments we have centred in our accounts of modernity – whether that be the American or French revolutions, or abolition of slavery across European empires – actually bear direct relations to what was going on in colonies such as Saint-Domingue.[24] Again, such link-building enables us to move beyond bifurcated accounts of history and the present in order to better understand – through our relational, Southern standpoint – the necessary connections between processes across the world, while also giving a deep recognition of agency to those colonized people. Staying with the example of the Haitian revolution, for instance, we can tease out more links to its relation to other events which we centre in our accounts of modernity. Scholars, for instance, have pointed out that the Haitian revolution itself was essential for the French revolution to play out as it did.[25] As Laurent Dubois (2004: 18) argues, Saint-Domingue was one of France's most prolific colonies due to its high production and exporting of sugar – 'the economic miracle of the eighteenth century' – and in that respect was the economic backbone of the French revolutionary state.

Furthermore, we can also think about the significance of the Haitian revolution for actions in the wider field outside of the French empire. Du Bois (2007 [1947]), for instance, highlights how decades before the Haitian revolution reached fruition, the people of this colony were already fostering a revolutionary spirit through directly supporting the 1779 revolution in the United States, joining forces against the British imperialists. Again, therefore, we have a relational or connected understanding which links centred events in modernity – such as the American revolution – with processes silenced in our sociological understandings of modernity (Bhambra 2007). Furthermore, as Du Bois (2007 [1947]) shows, the success of the Haitian revolution sent a shock wave through the colonies, with the Cuban and Dominican revolts following in 1794, as well as revolts and rebellions in Jamaica, St Lucia, Barbados, Brazil and Bolivia (again, with the assistance of Haitians). These revolts and rebellions – rather than a change towards benign attitudes in the metropoles themselves – were what pushed the empires towards abolishing slavery; they realized it was becoming more of an economic threat than a benefit to their systems of capital accumulation.[26] Again, therefore, by going beyond bifurcations typical of sociological understandings of modernity, we can both improve our historical accuracy about these processes and, in doing so, centre the previously invisiblized agency of those in the Global South.

Of course, recognizing the agency of colonized people or people in the Global South through the Southern standpoint does not necessitate only a reimagining of world history – it can also be achieved by different sociological methods. This is well exemplified by Jomo Kenyatta's (1979 [1938]) *Facing Mount Kenya*, in what can be understood as an early example of British ethnographic sociology.[27] Kenyatta came from Kenya to Britain in 1931, in order to study under Malinowski at the London School of Economics. Rather than reproduce the colonial episteme that was being manufactured in the imperial metropoles, *Facing Mount Kenya* is a perfect example of how the Southern standpoint directly opposes central tenets of the colonial episteme that was being practised in sociology. Kenyatta's ethnography looks at the organization and social practices of the Gikuyu people in central Kenya. From the very first page of this study, Kenyatta already attempts to shift the representation of such people away from the lens of the colonial episteme. In a footnote in his preface, therefore, Kenyatta (1979 [1938]: xv) brings attention to the way that, rather than 'Gikuyu', 'The usual European way of spelling the word is Kikuyu, which is incorrect; it should be Gikuyu, or in strict phonetic spelling Gekoyo.' In this respect, Kenyatta is already showing the need for a reflexivity which gives local people's (or 'ethnographic subjects") knowledge primacy in the research process – much in the same way that Du Bois (1898) had earlier criticized 'car window sociologists' who conduct ethnography without having any appreciation of the local knowledges which they are trying to study.

Furthermore, Kenyatta then directly confronts another dimension of the colonial episteme that we discussed in the previous chapter – the idea that those in the colonies were civilizationally 'backward', or a form of 'contemporaneous ancestry' (Thomas 1909: 146). As we considered in Giddings' (1898) work, one way that colonial rule was justified was through the idea that the empires were bringing civilization to these unruly places, particularly through the instigation of supposedly democratic political organizations. However, as Kenyatta (1979 [1938]) shows, democratic political organization was actually practised by the Gikuyu people prior to colonial intervention.[28] Thus, in chapter IX of *Facing Mount Kenya*, Kenyatta (1979 [1938]) focuses on 'The Gikuyu System of Government'. He points out that prior to colonial rule, the Gikuyu had a constitutional government – *njama ya itwika* – with every village appointing a representative to a Council that was responsible for drafting this constitution. This Council enshrined in law a series of principles which – had they been drafted centuries later by the French revolutionary council – would be seen as indicative of modern thought, such as:

1. Freedom for people to acquire and develop land through family ownership.
2. Universal tribal membership.
3. Abolition of the status of king and nobleman.
4. Government constituted by the Council, in turn chosen from all members of the community.
5. In order to avoid autocracy, election for government positions on a rotational basis.

These laws and political practices highlighted by Kenyatta, among many others, show that the Eurocentric standpoint of the colonial episteme was simply false. While sociologists were keen to reproduce the civilizational backwardness thesis of colonized people, Kenyatta adopted a different standpoint – a Southern standpoint – which allowed him to see far beyond the sociological studies which merely reproduced myths of colonial difference.

Indeed, in doing so Kenyatta also countered another dimension of the colonial episteme popular in sociology: the idea that the colonies were more 'simplistic' in their organization than the metropoles. It was precisely for this reason – that the colonies were not just backward, but 'simple' – that sociologists identified value in studying them. As Keller (1906: 417) stated:

The student who would understand the framework of society is led from the outset to the contemplation of its simplest forms. [...] Hence we find the work of a Spencer or Tylor concerning itself primarily with societies which lead relatively the simplest existence i.e. societies of so-called 'natives'. [...] Study of such societies gives us our only starting-points for the scientific demonstration of the evolution of human institutions.

In contrast to the standpoint within this colonial episteme, Kenyatta makes two interrelated points. Firstly, there is the straightforward idea that any simplicity in the organization of the colonies is the result of colonization – hence his criticism of how colonialism destroyed the Gikuyu's indigenous form of democratic government. Secondly, Kenyatta's whole book is itself dedicated to the various ways that the Gikuyu people maintain degrees of social practice with highly interconnected levels of complexity, which – going beyond the colonial episteme – can in no way be evidence of the Gikuyu living in a 'simple' society. For instance, Kenyatta highlights how the rituals and practices in magic – while being seen as primitive by European colonialists – directly interrelate with the Gikuyu's economic base. The Gikuyu people run a system where land belongs 'privately' to each family, but because the whole Gikuyu economy relies on land cultivation, these families always see their land practices as a collaborative, community-based exercise and societal duty. Magic feeds into this economic *mode of production*, in that the idea of individualism and opting out of one's group is seen as an example of evil magic. In this regard, the moralism of magic is not evidence of something that is primitive or simplistic, but rather is a practice and belief that fits directly into the overall running of the Gikuyu economic and social system. In this example alone, therefore, we see a highly complex relationship between economy, magic and group membership – a level of complexity which we can only capture through the Southern standpoint, which itself goes beyond the myopia of the colonial episteme.

A Southern standpoint beyond opposition?

Kenyatta's work, therefore, brings us back to the beginning of the chapter. The colonial episteme practised within sociology can itself be characterized as a standpoint – a Eurocentric standpoint. Through its Orientalism and/or bifurcated thinking, this Eurocentric standpoint results in sociological theories and research which are at best partial, and at worst an uncritical reproduction of colonial knowledge. In contrast to this, a sociology that embraces a Southern standpoint is able to transcend Orientalism and bifurcation, instead embracing a relational sociology that gives critical recognition and valuation to the agency of people in the Global South.

However, this new binary between the Eurocentric and Southern standpoints, the colonial and decolonial epistemes, gives rise to another problem in decolonizing sociology. Namely, if we define the Southern standpoint in virtue of its opposition to the Eurocentric standpoint or colonial episteme, do we not simply recentre that very system of thought whose hegemony we are seeking to displace? Through defining the Southern standpoint in terms of its resistance to the colonial episteme, we are only able to incorporate sociological knowledge that is itself in opposition to the colonial episteme, rather than sociological knowledge which is also *outside of* this episteme. In a sense, therefore, this leaves us in a position akin to a 'Eurocentric critique of Eurocentrism' (Grosfoguel 2017: 158) in the way that the colonial episteme remains the centre which alternative modes of thought are positioned against. Such an oppositional model neglects the idea that anything can exist outside or independently of this colonial episteme.

It is because of this need to highlight systems of thought that exist outside of the colonial episteme that decolonial thinkers have attempted to build autonomous sociologies, or to indigenize sociology. The extent to which such thinkers have succeeded in their aims is the topic of the following chapter.

Further reading

Articles

Alatas, Syed Farid, and Vineeta Sinha. 2001. 'Teaching Classical Sociological Theory in Singapore: The Context of Eurocentrism'. *Teaching Sociology* 29 (3): 316–31.

Syed Farid Alatas and Vineeta Sinha's paper reflects on their own experiences of teaching classical social theory – especially the likes of Weber, Durkheim and Marx – in the Global South context of Singapore. They suggest ways of critiquing the Orientalism and bifurcation in these thinkers' works, while also showing how parts of their social thought still remain useful. Alatas and Sinha thus show that decolonial sociology is often about forming conversations, rather than disregarding the work of any 'classical' author.

Go, Julian. 2016. 'Globalizing Sociology, Turning South: Perspectival Realism and the Southern Standpoint'. *Sociologica* 2: 1–42.

In this paper, Julian Go outlines what he terms 'the Southern standpoint'. In what Go theorizes as perspectival realism, this paper shows how the Southern standpoint is defined as being a position in the field of imperial relations, rather than being an essential identity. Through this paper, therefore, Go encourages us to consider how various standpoints have shaped sociology, and how the Southern standpoint in particular can advance sociological knowledge.

Patel, Sujata. 2014. 'Afterword: Doing Global Sociology: Issues, Problems and Challenges'. *Current Sociology* 62 (4): 603–13.

In this paper, Sujata Patel offers a critique of the Eurocentrism of mainstream sociology. At the same time, Patel critiques how – in the name of decolonization – many intellectual traditions in postcolonies (such as India) went down the route of a methodological nationalism, thus sociologically studying the nation state in isolation from its international relations. Patel's paper thus highlights what it would mean to at once provincialize European social thought and also form a global sociology that does not propagate its own universalism.

Books

Bhambra, Gurminder K. 2007. *Rethinking Modernity: Postcolonialism and the Sociological Imagination.* London: Palgrave Macmillan.

Gurminder K. Bhambra's book discusses how dominant social scientists have understood the process of modernity, what they have excluded in these understandings, and what these exclusions can tell us about the wider framing of Western society. Bhambra succinctly analyses how processes of colonialism, enslavement, land expropriation and the formation of empires, as well as historical events such as the Haitian revolution, are absent from social scientific accounts of modernity.

Mignolo, Walter. 2011. *The Darker Side of Western Modernity: Global Futures, Decolonial Options.* Durham, NC: Duke University Press.

Like Bhambra's book, Mignolo's analyses how colonialism acted as a big bang for European modernity. In this analysis, Mignolo develops the concept of 'modernity/coloniality', looking at the material and epistemic interrelation between the two processes. Mignolo's book then highlights how decolonial thought can emerge from the borders of this modern, colonial world system, and how the issue of decoloniality necessarily requires a struggle for epistemic justice.

–2–
Beyond Intellectual Imperialism: Indigenous and Autonomous Sociologies

From the previous chapter, we have the idea that much canonical sociology has a clouded, or partial, standpoint. This does not mean to say that the work of canonical sociologists ought to be dismissed, but rather that their work ought to be historicized correctly, and – as per all sociological work – scrutinized with a degree of healthy scepticism (after all, no work ought to be immune to critique). However, what exacerbates the problem of having a 'partial' or clouded sociological canon is that despite its flaws, this Western canon is exported as being *the* universal model of sociology to the rest of the world. Needless to say, the exporting of this canon across the world has been contested from varying decolonial positions. This had led decolonial sociologists to stress the need to connect with, and build upon, *indigenous* or *autonomous* sociologies. This chapter thus engages with why such sociologists have called for these alternative ways of doing sociology, the benefits and drawbacks of going 'autonomous' or 'indigenous', and some examples of this thought in practice.

Launching the canon across the globe

In the introduction to this book, I discussed the history of how sociology developed in the metropoles. This history of sociology has led many – including decolonial social scientists themselves – to argue that sociology was '"invented" by Western scholarship and [...] evolved in response to discrete problems in the developed countries which nurtured them', thus meaning that sociology 'generally [...] stayed at home' in its analysis (Gareau 1988: 171–2). By contrast, this chapter highlights how just as sociology was developing in the metropoles, it was also developing in the Global South (often being institutionalized by colonial powers which had set up universities in their colonies).

Take, for instance, Patrick Geddes, who was previously mentioned as one of the founding fathers of British sociology in the early twentieth century. Not only was Geddes a supposed founding figure of sociology in Britain, but he also held the first sociology professorship in India, at the University of Bombay, between 1919 and 1923.[1] Indeed, as Patel (2017) has shown, India had as many institutions teaching sociology in the early twentieth century as Britain did itself, if not more. Geddes' professorship at the University of Bombay, however, was not very well received by the Indian students who wanted to learn sociology. Instead of teaching issues that engaged the students, as Helen Meller (2005) has shown in her biography of Geddes, he either attempted to indoctrinate his students with the 'civics' approach he had formerly developed in Britain, or, indeed, recommended his students go to Britain to be trained in sociology.

This anecdote about Geddes' time in India helps illustrate two key points developed in this chapter. Firstly, this chapter highlights that sociology was developing in the Global South at the very same time that it was developing in the metropoles. While much of this sociology *in* the Global South was really a Eurocentric sociology *of* the Global South, there were still developing autonomous, critical paradigms of thought which contemporary sociologists are now drawing upon. It is therefore not accurate to suppose that sociology only developed in the US and Europe as a US and European enterprise. Secondly, as per the experience of Geddes' students, since the development of sociology in the Global South, there have been numerous examples of Southern intellectuals rejecting the universality of Western theory.

Given these realities that there are critical sociological traditions from the Global South, and that Southern intellectuals have rejected the universality of Western sociology, it is no surprise that over the years we have seen Southern sociologists call for developing indigenous and/or autonomous sociologies. In order to contextualize these calls, we must understand sociology's role in supporting the coloniality of knowledge and a global epistemicide, both of which have led to a continuing 'intellectual imperialism'.

The coloniality of knowledge, global epistemicide and intellectual imperialism

The coloniality of knowledge concerns the 'impact of colonization on the different areas of knowledge production' (Maldonado-Torres 2007: 242). The impact of colonization on knowledge production has been the creation of an epistemic hierarchy 'that privileges Western knowledge and cosmology over non-Western knowledge and cosmologies [which was then] institutionalized in the global university system' (Grosfoguel 2007: 217). Through the coloniality of knowledge, therefore, sociology has partaken in what Boaventura de Sousa Santos (2014) refers to as a global epistemicide – an erasure of 'other' ways and forms of knowing and knowledge that differ from those of the supposedly superior West. A consequence of this epistemicide is that through erasing 'other' knowledges, sociologists in the Global North are now 'disabled [...] from learning in noncolonial terms, that is, in terms that allow for the existence of histories other than the universal history of the West' (Santos 2014: 19). Furthermore, erasing systems of knowledge from the South additionally 'involves the destruction of the social practices and the disqualification of the social agents that operate according to such knowledges' living in the South (Santos 2014: 153). In other words, the epistemicide that sociology supported through colonialism, and now through the coloniality of knowledge, not only devalues *knowledge* from the South, but in doing so, devalues the very existence of those people that constructed those knowledge systems.

Through devaluing Southern knowledges, Western sociology is then presented to the South as a universal canon which can fill their lacunae of scholarly sociological work. This creates a relationship that Syed Farid Alatas (1993, 2003) and Syed Hussein Alatas (2000) term 'intellectual imperialism'. Just as imperialism, broadly defined, refers to a 'strategy of political control over foreign lands' (Steinmetz 2014: 79), S. H. Alatas (2000) argues that intellectual imperialism refers especially to control over a foreign region's intellectual production, in this case, specifically the Global North's control over the intellectual production of the Global South. This relationship of intellectual imperialism is sustained not necessarily by economic or military intervention, but rather through the functioning of the overall transnational political economy of knowledge production.[2] The Global North rationalizes its intellectual imperialism, as the whole political economy of knowledge is shaped to benefit the Global North through the infrastructure of university rankings, funding councils, journals, academic publishers, conference proceedings and so on.[3] Sociology is not exempt from this intellectual imperialism, and in fact is a perfect example of such inequality in practice. Moreover, this intellectual imperialism sustained by sociology is not just a new phenomenon, but has been a part of sociology since its formal emergence.

Intellectual imperialism: Intellectual imperialism describes the process through which the knowledge production of one territory is partially controlled by another. Thinkers such as Syed Hussein Alatas (2000) and Frederick Gareau (1988) have used the notion of intellectual imperialism to highlight how sociologists in the Global South are often forced to study their own societies through theoretical paradigms developed in the Global North – even when such paradigms are not fit for purpose.

The past and present of sociology's intellectual imperialism

As discussed in the aforementioned example of Geddes, Meller (2005) highlights that one of the features of his professorship was recommending that his top students go to Britain to be trained in sociology. Geddes' recommendation, in this respect, is a typical example of intellectual imperialism: sociologists in the South must be trained in Northern institutions in order to be recognized as sociologists in the global academic community. This intellectual imperialism meant that across the Global South, where sociology was becoming institutionalized in universities, Southern intellectuals who wanted to teach at these universities often had to be trained in the metropoles, and, in consequence, were largely trained in the theory and methods of colonial sociology. Argentina, for example, is an interesting case because it had its first chair in sociology appointed in 1898 at UBA School of Philosophy and Letters, and thus the discipline developed on a similar timeline to that in the United States (Pereyra 2010).[4] However, because of the intellectual imperialism which stressed the requirement of Northern training, one of the supposed 'founders' of Argentinian sociology – Gino Germani – was himself trained at the University of Rome and Harvard University before making a significant contribution to sociology in Argentina (Pereyra 2010). By similar logic, Tina Uys (2010) shows that in South Africa, two of the leading proponents of sociology – Edward Baston and Geoffrey Cronjé – were trained at the London School of Economics and the University of Amsterdam respectively, while in India, as Patel (2010) shows, the 'father of Indian sociology', M. A. Ghurye, was educated at Cambridge University before he became a recognized sociologist at Bombay University.

Furthermore, given that these 'first figures' of sociology often had to be trained in the North, this allowed for another facet of intellectual imperialism: the reproduction of Northern theories by/in Southern institutions. To use previous examples, Geoffrey Cronjé became a professor of sociology in 1936 at the University of Pretoria, having achieved his PhD in sociology and criminology from the University of Amsterdam. However, in his professorship, Cronjé did not seek to develop any kind of critical or autonomous 'South African' sociology, but rather borrowed from European understandings of racial hierarchy to argue that South Africa was naturally divided by race, and needed to separate the inferior races from mixing with whites; thus he has earned the label of being the 'mind of apartheid'.[5] Similarly M. A. Ghurye, having gained his doctorate at Cambridge University, did not form a critical, anti-imperial sociology at Bombay University.[6] Instead, as Patel (2010) shows, Ghurye's sociology developed the British focus on caste in India, encouraging his students to research the particular traditions and rituals of each caste, and in doing so not only reified the caste system imposed by British colonialism, but also strengthened the myth of Brahmin supremacy which continues today. In both cases, therefore, the strength of intellectual imperialism meant that Southern institutions and intellectuals were not necessarily producing critical 'Southern theory', but were reproducing the colonial episteme.

Indeed, this episteme could easily be reproduced in the Global South because the colonizing empires *controlled* most of these universities. Furthermore, even as former colonies became formally independent, the metropoles still exerted large degrees of control over their education systems.[7] This intellectual imperialism thus allowed for prominent sociologists in 'superior' Northern institutions to spend time as chairs in sociology at universities in former colonies, and to disseminate their theories in these new locales. An example of this is Norbert Elias, a German-British sociologist seen as the pioneer of 'relational' sociology, who became chair of sociology at the University of Ghana in 1961 (Ghana became independent in 1957). Elias is perhaps most known for his work on the 'civilizing process', where he tracks how Europe became civilized after the Middle Ages, when the state and bourgeois institutions sought to better enforce formal behaviour between different members of society (Elias 1982 [1939]). I hope that by now your decolonial antennae are already sending off signals at this mention of 'civilizing process', especially given the fact that Elias locates this process as happening in Europe rather than anywhere else in the world. Upon becoming a chair of sociology at the University of Ghana, and arguing that he was going to produce the first sociological – rather than anthropological – study of Ghanaians, Elias did *not* find any civilizing process in Ghana, but rather contrasted the free and emotive-driven lives of the Ghanaians with the formal civilizing process seen in Europe (see Goody 2003).

In this respect, we see again how intellectual imperialism allowed sociologists such as Elias to not revise their theories, but merely reproduce them in the South. In colonialism, and the immediate 'postcolonial' period, therefore, sociology partook in an epistemicide that resisted the production of sociological systems counter to Northern, hegemonic ways of thinking. While Sall and Ouedraogo (2010: 226) are thus speaking about sociology across West Africa, their analysis holds for sociology and colonialism more generally, when they comment that:

> sociology under colonialism became a science in the service of the colonial order, whose main purpose was to study African societies to further the colonial project. In the colonial context, it was unthinkable for the natives to have had any desire to study their own societies

outside the political prescriptions of the colonial order
– otherwise there would have been no need for the
civilizing mission of colonialism. Just as colonialism
recruited locals for its armies, this science used 'native'
auxiliaries and informants to create knowledge about
the 'other'. In the process, it undermined local power
structures and institutions and devalued all competing
modes of knowing and thinking to be termed as
'magical' and 'pre-logical', and having no claims to
scientificity. This page of African history left a lasting
imprint on the African elite, many of whom were
trained in European universities and used the languages
of the former colonial masters.

Importantly in this quote from Sall and Ouedraogo, the
authors bring attention to the 'lasting imprint' of the epistemicide and intellectual imperialism that sociology partook in
during colonialism. It is especially important to shed light
upon this lasting imprint, given that many contemporary
sociologists are still describing similar realities to what we
have been describing in terms of sociology in colonial and
immediately postcolonial societies. In Iran, for instance, Ali
Shari'ati (1986: 32) criticized the rise of pseudo-intellectuals,
who went to the West for academic training before coming
back to Iran with the mission 'to make people "modern"
and assimilate the elites and the progressive educated youth
of non-European societies into European culture inside their
own traditional societies and, hence, establish a base for
Western penetration and arrival'. By similar logic, S. F. Alatas
(2000) made the same points about intellectuals in Singapore
and Malaysia. Furthermore, unlike the formative years of
sociology, it is also worth bringing attention to how from
the 1960s through to the twenty-first century much social
science in the Global South has been funded by Western-led
non-governmental organizations (NGOs), and institutions
such as the World Bank and International Monetary Fund,
and how this social science – despite supposedly good intentions – often ends up searching for ways to 'develop' the rest

of the world according to Western ideals of neoliberalism.[8] This critique of Western-led NGO-funded research has been made in the context of sociology in a wide range of places across the Global South, including Palestine (Hanafi 2010), West Africa (Sall and Ouedraogo 2010), and Latin America (Briceño-León 2010; Bringel and Domingues 2017).

More than a hundred years since its beginnings, therefore, sociology continues to operate according to a logic of intellectual imperialism. A central component of intellectual imperialism today is the epistemic division within sociology – born in colonialism – whereby the South is incorporated into the research focus, but the *theory* still comes from the North (Connell et al. 2018). If we think about all of the sociologists who are globally canonized in social theory – for instance, Marx, Weber, Durkheim, Bourdieu, Foucault – they tend to be thinkers from the Global North.[9] However, each of these social theorists relied on 'data' from the South: Marx and Weber both gathered material on China and India to contrast these 'Asiatic' societies and religions with Western society (Marx 1853; Zimmerman 2006), and Bourdieu's theory of practice was based on his research in the Kabyle (Puwar 2009; Steinmetz 2014), while Foucault's thoughts on power developed through his encounters with revolutionaries in Tunisia (Medien 2019). Critics have highlighted this continuing epistemic division in sociology, as third-sector organizations, research councils, and universities in the Global North continue to fund projects on the Global South – such as on the topics of HIV or climate change – with the theoretical 'discoveries' and 'interventions' being credited to the Global North (see Connell et al. 2017, 2018). As S. H. Alatas (2000: 25) thus highlights, intellectual imperialism – including the epistemic division between theory and data in the North and South – follows precisely the same pattern as other forms of imperialism that we typically think of:

In political and economic imperialism, the mother country exploited the raw materials of the colonies. They brought the raw materials back to the mother country, manufactured the product in the mother country, and then distributed the products in the colonies. The colonies were regarded as sources for raw materials as well as markets for the industrial products of the mother country. A clear example for us is rubber. Rubber was grown in Malaya, latex was taken to England, tyres were made in England, and then were sold here. [...] Data is from this region, raw data on certain topics are collected in this region, processed and manufactured in England in the form of books or articles, and then sold here. On the whole, people of this region including their scholars were used mainly as informants. We are continuously bombarded by foreign publications. [...] They came here, gathered the raw intellectual materials, went back, published their books, and exported the finished product back to the country of fieldwork.

Intellectual imperialism has thus been part and parcel of sociological knowledge production since its beginning days. However, perhaps more so than in previous periods, sociologists of recent years have begun to collectively examine the precise consequences of intellectual imperialism for those doing sociology in the Global South. This has led to two theories: the captive mind theory and the theory of extraversion.

Theorizing the captive mind and extraversion

The 'captive mind' theory was popularized by S. H. Alatas (2000) and S. F. Alatas (2000, 2003, 2014), in order to explain the conditions of social scientists working in the Global South and their overall relationship to intellectual production in the metropoles. Central to the captive mind theory is that the global political economy of knowledge production – much like the economic realities of the later twentieth century – is characterized by a relationship of Southern dependency on the North. As Alatas (2003: 602) clarifies: 'The West's monopolistic control of and influence over the social sciences in much of the Third World are not determined in the first instance by force via colonial power but rather by the dependence of Third World scholars and intellectuals on western social science in a variety of ways.' Alatas (2003: 604–5) then went on to divide this Southern academic dependency into six types:

1. *Dependency on ideas*: In this form of dependency, Alatas argues that social scientists working in the Global South tend to rely on theories imported from the Global North: 'In both teaching and research knowledge at all these levels overwhelmingly originates from the US and the UK and, in the case of the former French colonies, France. There is hardly any original metatheoretical or theoretical analysis emerging from the Third World.'

2. *Dependency in the media of ideas*: Here, Alatas argues that the Global North controls the publishing infrastructure that is central to the global field of academia: 'The degree of academic dependency in this case can be gauged from the structure of ownership and control of publishing houses, journals, working paper series and websites.'

3. *Dependency for technology*: Here, Alatas highlights how the most 'advanced' technology (such as software and research equipment) is often donated to institutions in the Global South for data collection.

4. *Dependency on aid from the Global North*: In this comment, Alatas sheds light on how the Global North often provides funds to the Global South in order 'to sponsor research, purchase books and other instructional materials, finance the publication of local books and journals, and buy expertise in the form of visiting scholars'.

5. *Dependency in education*: Here, Alatas sheds light on how universities in the Global North exert control over not just research but also teaching in the Global South: 'This refers to the direct investment of educational institutions from the West in the Third World. An example would be the various degree programmes offered by North American, British and Australian universities in Asia, sometimes involving joint ventures with local organizations. Without

such direct investment, there would be fewer opportunities for tertiary education and fewer teaching jobs available in Asian countries.'

6. *Dependency in terms of brain drain*: Lastly, Alatas claims that intellectuals in the Global South have a dependency on the North in order to be recognized as experts in their respective discipline. In other words, they must be recognized as experts by those in the Global North before they are officially recognized as experts in the global academic field. As Alatas thus highlights: 'Third World scholars become dependent on demand for their expertise in the West. The brain drain may not necessarily result in the physical relocation of these scholars in the West. In cases where there is no physical relocation, there is still a brain drain in terms of the using up of mental resources and energy for research projects conceived in the West but which employ Third World personnel as junior research partners.'

Starting from the recognition of this relationship of academic dependency, both S. H. Alatas (2000) and S. F. Alatas (1993, 2000) argue that this dependency causes intellectuals in the Global South to demonstrate a condition these authors describe as the 'captive mind'. At the foundation of this theory is that the captive mind is characterized by those in the South adopting an 'uncritical and imitative [...] approach to ideas and concepts from the West' (Alatas 1993: 29). Building on this base-level understanding of the captive mind, S. F. Alatas (2000) thus argued that the captive mind, common to academics working in the Global South, features eight characteristics:

1. An uncritical imitation of Western thought.
2. An uncreative method of thinking that cannot raise original problems.
3. A method of thinking that relies on stereotypes of the Global South created by the Global North.
4. An inability to separate 'particular' theories from universal theories.

5. A fragmented viewpoint.
6. Understandings and theories imported from the Global North which are alienated from the major issues of the society being studied in the South.
7. A separation from its own intellectual pursuit.
8. Being unconscious of its own captivity.

Central to the captive mind theory, therefore, is the idea that the current phase of coloniality is typified by a 'Western domination' of intellectual production across the globe. This domination results not only in military and economic intervention in the Global South, but also in direct and indirect academic intervention in and control over the Global South, thus resulting in a continuing epistemicide that resists the production of independent Southern thought. In this regard, the notion of mental captivity connects with decolonial Kenyan writer Ngũgĩ wa Thiong'o's (1987: 16) claim that 'economic and political control can never be complete or effective without mental control'. As S. F. Alatas (2000) states, however, this mental domination is not just imposed by a foreign power, but is also reproduced by the dominated themselves, in their state of internalized oppression. This internalized oppression – to use the language of Shari'ati (1986) – creates a 'one-dimensional' intellectual, with no diversity of thought being formed across the dominant academic field.

However, it is precisely in this notion of internalized oppression that we can see the drawbacks to the captive mind theory. One of the foundational points of decolonial thought – in sociology and beyond – is the notion that those in the Global South have agency. While S. H. Alatas (2013 [1977]) and S. F. Alatas (2014) have both dedicated their intellectual careers to demonstrating this decolonial tenet, their theory of the captive mind contrastingly makes it appear as though intellectuals in the Global South have no agency; such intellectuals merely become uncritical mouthpieces for the Global North. It is for this reason that decolonial thinkers, as per Paulin Hountondji's (1997) call, may prefer to explore the theory of *extraversion* over the theory of the captive mind.

Through this move towards extraversion, we can see that it is too simplistic to describe the relationship between academics in the Global South and North as one of mental captivity. Instead, extraversion highlights the strategies that those in the South develop in order to navigate a global political economy of knowledge in which the North consistently attempts to reproduce its hegemony.

Like the captive mind theory, the theory of extraversion also admits that the global political economy of knowledge is marked by intellectual imperialism. In this respect, Hountondji (1997), one of the prominent extraversion theorists, describes the political economy of knowledge in a similar way to how it is described by those supporting the captive mind theory. As Hountondji therefore states, the political economy of knowledge is characterized by the following features:

1. Scientific work in the Global South depends on the 'use of apparatus imported from the centre' (Hountondji 1997: 7).
2. The Southern 'intellectual work is to a large extent dependent on journals, libraries, archives, publishing houses and other support facilities in the North', meaning that even the new journals emerging in the South have a larger readership and more contributors from the North than South (Hountondji 1997: 7). The case of Israel illustrates this point. As Azarya (2010: 250) shows, the Hebrew University ranking of journals for sociology is a criterion used to evaluate Israeli sociologists, and yet, according to this ranking, 'the top A category includes thirteen periodicals, none of which is published in the Hebrew language nor does it even include an English language Israeli publication'.
3. Southern intellectuals are better known in the North than in the South, thus explaining why, for instance, many classical sociologists in Europe such as Comte and Gumplowicz recognized Ibn Khaldūn as a sociologist before his work was taken up in Southern sociology (as argued in Alatas 2006).
4. While Northern researchers can be as global as they want,

Southern research tends to be based on the scholar's immediate, local environment.

5. Southern research, as opposed to Northern theoretical work, tends to be driven by a policy-creating agenda. This perhaps helps explain why much sociology conducted *on* the Global South, since the discipline's creations, has been funded by various governmental and non-governmental organizations in search of policy formation, such as the colonial offices of Britain and France (Steinmetz 2017), UNESCO (Steinmetz 2013) and the World Bank (Sall and Ouedraogo 2010).

6. The brain drain from South to North means that not only do Southern intellectuals attempt to move to Northern institutions, but they are also driven in one way or the other 'towards the centre of the system' in terms of where they publish, who they cite, where they do institutional visits and which conferences they attend (Hountondji 1997: 9). For instance, while we now have national sociological associations in places such as India, the Philippines, South Korea, Pakistan, Australia and New Zealand (Dufoix 2018), organizations such as the American Sociological Association and the International Sociological Association (which claims to be international but is run by North-majority committees) remain hegemonic (Burawoy 2015).

7. Southern thinkers have to travel North for research centres, conferences and advanced courses in a form of 'scientific tourism', while Northern thinkers are not required to go South.

8. When Northern thinkers 'go South', they tend to be in 'search not of knowledge but only of materials that lead to knowledge and, if need be, to a testing ground for their findings. They do not go searching for paradigms or methodological and theoretical models; rather, they go hunting for information and new facts that are likely to enrich their paradigms' (Hountondji 1997: 11). Again, this refers to the epistemic divide in sociology, where the Global South provides a pool of data for Northern theory.

9. Courses and publications in the Global South still tend to regularly use imperial languages, while in order to publish

in journals and university presses outside of the Global South, fluency in these imperial languages is a prerequisite. This can perhaps be represented in the recent case where Elsevier, owner of multiple academic journals, recommended to contributors that they ought not to cite sources which are not published in English.[10]

Unlike the captive mind theorists, however, those from the extraversion standpoint do not necessarily go along with the premise that Southern intellectuals uncritically reproduce this structure of dependency. Instead, the theory of extraversion highlights how Southern intellectuals are aware of the imperial power structure within academia, and develop strategies to navigate through this unequal world. Thus, rather than the concept of 'captivity' and non-agency highlighted in the captive mind theory, extraversion ought to be seen as:

a pattern of agency, *a way of dealing with a collective situation in the global economy of knowledge*. This is not a position of powerlessness. The economy of knowledge needs a workforce in the periphery, given the global circulation of data, debate and applied science. (Connell et al. 2018: 54, emphasis added)

Through the theory of extraversion, therefore, we can see that Southern intellectuals publishing in Northern journals, writing in Northern languages and engaging with Northern theory are not uncritical mouthpieces for the North. These intellectual practices stem not from the *absence* of knowledge and critical thought, but rather from the *outcome* of critical reflection on the political economy of knowledge. Such critical reflection on sociology and the political economy of knowledge show that such strategies of engaging with the North remain the most viable for getting one's research done, given the reality that 'to function successfully as a [social] scientist one must read the leading journals published in the metropole, learn the research techniques taught there and gain recognition there. [...] The theoretical hegemony of the

North is simply the normal functioning of this economy of knowledge' (Connell et al. 2017: 51).

> **Extraversion**: Extraversion is a particular strategy for dealing with intellectual imperialism. As theorized by Paulin Hountondji (1997), extraversion is the process through which academics in the Global South position themselves relative to the Global North – whether that be by desiring to publish in Northern journals or manuscript publishers, attend prestigious conferences in the Global North, or receive renowned visiting fellowships at Northern institutions. As Connell et al. (2017, 2018) show, extraversion is thus a form of academic agency practised in the Global South to navigate Northern hegemony in the political economy of knowledge.

Of course, while extraversion and the captive mind are two rival theories, they are both offered to diagnose the same problem: intellectual imperialism steeped in the coloniality of knowledge. Just as, with colonialism and the coloniality of power more broadly, since there has been colonialism there has been decolonial thought, so in parallel, since there has been intellectual imperialism and a coloniality of knowledge within sociology there have been critical systems of thought that have sought to challenge this vision and practice of sociology. This is what leads scholars such as Connell (2011, 2018) to argue that one of the central missions of sociology is to bridge the gap that developed between sociology and critical social thought (in the past and present), and in doing so, broaden our ideas of what is encompassed under the wide umbrella of sociology and social theory to begin with. Such a mission to bridge that imperial gap between sociology and critical social thought has underlined other intellectuals' calls to build 'indigenous' or 'autonomous' sociologies.

Indigenous and autonomous sociology: decentring or
recentring Northern theory?

Given the coloniality of knowledge and epistemicide described
in this chapter, it is no surprise that these calls for indigenous
or autonomous sociology are rooted in the wider mission of
decolonizing sociology. Such calls realize that the battle for
decolonization takes place not only in political offices and
economic policies, but also on the epistemic terrain. Thus, as
Mignolo and Walsh (2018: 146) put it:

> Decoloniality is first and foremost liberation of
> knowledge [...] of understanding and affirming subjec-
> tivities that have been devalued by narratives of
> modernity that are constitutive of the CMP [colonial
> matrix of power]. Its main goal is the transformation
> of colonial subjects and subjectivities into decolonial
> subjects and subjectivities.

Part of forming decolonial knowledge, therefore, requires
taking 'seriously the epistemic perspective/cosmologies/
insights of critical thinkers from the Global South' (Grosfoguel
2007: 212). Since its beginnings in the South, sociologists
have sought to form such decolonial knowledge, although
this mission always remained marginal in the wider global
field of sociology. Both Patel (2010, 2016) and Bhambra
(2014), for instance, highlight the work of the Lucknow
School of Economics and Sociology in India, founded in
the 1920s under the leadership of Radhakamal Mukerjee
and D. P. Mukerji. As Patel and Bhambra show, the aim
of this school was to produce a 'spirit of self-reliance' and
original critical thought in social science that would connect
with anti-colonial work in other areas of Indian social life,
including Gandhi's work in the political sphere. Doing so,
Mukerjee and Mukerji believed, involved breaking with
using Eurocentric social science to analyse Indian society;
for instance, issues such as poverty in India simply could not
be analysed through concepts derived from a Western social

science that only understood these phenomena in the overall context of the industrial revolution (Patel 2016). While the Lucknow School was founded in the 1920s, it connects with the project – continuing in the present day – to build indigenous, or autonomous, sociologies.

Central to the project of indigenizing sociology is giving primacy to local ways and traditions of thinking and knowing. At a basic level, therefore, this indigenizing approach involves a societal reflexive look inward, searching for local explanations for local phenomena. In such a scenario, the idea is that sociologists in the South would not be faced with a situation such as Mukerjee and Mukerji were with the Lucknow School, as previously mentioned, where problems specific to the Indian locale, of poverty and destitution, were being analysed through Eurocentric concepts built for the study of European societies (Patel 2016). As Go (2016b: 10) comments, therefore, through indigenous sociology, the idea is that:

> rather than relying solely on a handful of theories from Northern theorists, this version of indigenous sociology urges sociologists to look elsewhere. [...] Instead of Max Weber for insights on the societies of the Middle East, we should instead turn to Abd al-Rahmān Ibn Khaldūn; or instead of just Karl Marx to think about Latin America, we might instead look at Simon Bolivar, Jose Martí, Octavio Paz or more recent thinkers like Nestor García Canclini. [...] Or rather than using Foucault to examine Indian society, we should heed the insights of Ashis Nandy or Benoy Kumar Sarkar.

A similar point to Go's was made by Jìmí Adésínà (2006) in the context of South Africa, where he proposes that sustaining an indigenous sociology is the best way to counter the nation's current crisis of what he terms a 'sociology of despair'. This sociology of despair, to Adésínà, has involved South African sociologists rejecting local knowledges in favour of an extraversion towards Northern theory. As

Adésínà (2006: 255) explains, this sociology of despair and extraversion has resulted in his calls for an 'African sociology' being met with confusion and bewilderment:

> Doing African Sociology rather than sociology in Africa does not seem to come easy to many of us [...] [I was presenting] an outline of what I referred to as African Sociology from the perspective of distilling epistemological guidelines from an African ontological narrative. My colleague listened attentively, paused for some time. He was puzzled ..., and then he said: 'But that won't be Sociology'. I asked, why not. His response was 'But where is Weber; where is Marx or Durkheim?'

As captured in this exchange, Adésínà highlights how indigenous epistemologies across Africa – through the sociology of despair – are rejected by sociologists *in* Africa, who favour the Western canon instead.

In order to build an indigenous sociology in the South African context, Adésínà thus argues that this would require:

1. A turn towards figures such as Steve Biko and Goven Mbeki, recognizing such intellectuals not only as political figures but as public sociologists.
2. Engaging with the work of classical South African sociologists, such as Bernard Magubane, Archie Mafeje and Fatima Meer.
3. Engaging with the work of contemporary South African sociologists, including Ari Sitas and Jeremy Skeekings.

Through these practices, Adésínà (2006: 257) proposes that South Africa can build a critical indigenous tradition of sociology, and indeed, that 'the same should apply to the works of African scholars on the rest of the continent'. Underlying the call for indigenous sociology is thus an idea that 'turning local' in order to explain local phenomena enables us to understand the society better than from the Eurocentric standpoint. Such local standpoints are given epistemic superiority because they are better situated in the local traditions and customs of thinking and knowing.

Take, for instance, the concept of agency – a theme we will return to in the final chapter when discussing the climate crisis and indigenous theories of the self and environment. The concept of agency has been central to debates in social theory in the metropole, with sociologists such as Pierre Bourdieu (1990a), Anthony Giddens (1984), Jürgen Habermas (1976), Ulrich Beck (2002), Margaret Archer (2003) and many more contemplating the relationship between agency (the individual) and structure (society and institutions). However, the very way that such Northern theory has defined and approached the concept of 'agency', as Go (2016a) shows, is through the notion of bourgeois individualism: an individual being able to act in accordance with their will, being completely unconstrained in such actions. Indigenizing sociology, by contrast, shows how this concept of agency does not work universally, as is captured in the works of Akinsola Akiwowo in the development of *Asuwada* epistemology.

Akinsola Akiwowo (1986, 1999) turned to the *Asuwada* epistemology, rooted in the Yoruba oral tradition, in order to explain the relationship between self and society which resulted in a radically different concept of agency from that theorized in the metropoles. This *Asuwada* epistemology, rather than giving a concept of agency as bourgeois individualism, actually shows how agency and individual identity are something that is achieved *through* – rather than in spite of – groups and structures (Akiwowo 1999). Thus, through this epistemology, the individual's worth is judged through group-based criteria including *ajumose* – the unity an individual expresses with their wider community – while the whole notion of *iwa* (good character) is rooted in participation in community, with *omoburuku* (bad person) being ascribed to those who self-alienate from their group and pursue a life of individualism.

As Omobowale and Akanle (2017: 45) thus show, this indigenous sociology gives us a radically different concept of agency from what we encounter in Northern theory, whereby:

> The individual is situated within a community where he exists and is also socially constructed into a social being. There exists therefore a symbiotic relationship between the individual and his community. [...] As much as each individual is unique, he requires the association of other interacting individuals to be socially whole and complete. Hence, the sanctity of the physical individual is rather meaningless without the community, as the essence of an individual lies within the community within which he exists. The physical and individual being must thus be transformed to a social being in order to be relevant in his/her society.

Through an indigenous approach to sociology, the aim is to highlight how Southern realities are not always able to be captured in Northern theories. Indigenizing sociology, therefore, not only involves broadening the concept of 'theory' to be more receptive to local epistemologies, but consequently also refers to indigenizing the sociological 'canon' more broadly across local contexts. This is the logic that underlies, as previously mentioned, Adésínà's (2006) call for South African sociologists to engage with the work of other South African sociologists. Of course, the link between widening the concept of theory and rebuilding new canons becomes quite clear in the indigenous sociology paradigm: once we extend the scope of the sociological umbrella to include new epistemologies and critical thought that Western sociology excluded, then we also start including thinkers who hitherto have not been considered as sociologists.

Nevertheless, while there is obvious value in indigenizing sociology, the call for such indigenization has been challenged. Firstly, there is the critique summarized by Bhambra (2014) that indigenous sociology often involves repackaging Western concepts in Southern concepts and/or language. To take the aforementioned example of Akiwowo and *Asuwada* epistemology, for instance, critics such as Ifeanyi Onwuzuruigbo (2018) have questioned whether Akiwowo was really sculpting an indigenous sociology or simply looking for Yoruba equivalents to terms such as 'agency', or Western-defined social problems such as the self and society. In such a case, then, indigenous sociology would really just be a case of indigenous variations of Western sociology and, in being so, would merely maintain 'the West' as the sociological nucleus.

Secondly, there is the connected critique from Go (2016b) that indigenizing sociology focuses so much on local epistemologies and traditions that it ceases to be sociological in the first place. As Michael Burawoy (2010) adds, this is not a critique of the value of such epistemologies, but rather a critique of whether producing indigenous knowledge – that is, producing knowledge on local society using local epistemologies – fulfils the sociological mission to produce theories that can be used across a variety of different settings. As Go (2016b: 12) thus comments: 'How do Yoruban concepts unearthed from deep oral traditions help us grasp the global logics of capitalist domination? How can theories or concepts derived from particular local contexts speak to global social processes?' Moreover, through this focus on localism, indigenizing sociology also faces the issue of claiming any epistemic privileges; namely, those who support indigenizing sociology often start from the premise that Western social science is itself indigenous to the West, and thus cannot be easily imported into the South. Yet, as Go (2016b: 12) shows, this logic potentially puts indigenous sociology into a difficulty, given that 'if Anglo-European social theory falls short because of its provinciality, would not indigenous sociology suffer from the exact same problem?'

One of the responses to this problem posed by Go is for supporters of indigenizing sociology to thus argue for a 'mosaic' of sociological knowledge, where each indigenous tradition is seen as equally suitable for analysing its own society (see Connell 2010). Once again, through dismissing the perspective of the 'god's eye' – that is, of claiming universal knowledge – such a mosaic approach to socio-logical knowledge allows us to move beyond the idea of a superior sociological system that must be imported across the world, as per the dictum of intellectual imperialism (Connell 2018). However, as Connell (2010) argues, even within this 'mosaic' model, we can still see how what we really get is a Western centre, with 'indigenous' sociologies building a mosaic *around* this imperial core. This is because such a mosaic model makes it appear as though indig-enous approaches are all separate from one another, lacking connections and conversations with one another, such that 'indigenous knowledge is treated as a fixed set of concepts and beliefs, rooted in tradition, to be defended against outside pressures for change' (Connell 2010: 44). As Connell (2010) shows, treating indigenous knowledge as closed in this way thus reproduces the very colonial logic we are trying to work against; indigenous thought gets dismissed or devalued as pre-modern, or traditional, rather than being seen as the critical social theory that it actually is.

It is precisely because of these criticisms to do with the sociology of knowledge that other intellectuals have instead called for 'autonomous' sociologies. In particular, both S. H. Alatas (2006) and S. F. Alatas (2000, 2003) have developed the call for 'autonomous sociology', which they both deem to be superior to the call for indigenizing sociology. Indeed, if we look at S. H. Alatas' (2006) argument, then he actually starts from the premise that the whole concept of 'indigenous sociology' does not make sense. As he argues:

> There should not be an indigenization of the social sciences because the concept of indigenization does not apply to the sciences. What applies is the result of the scientific approach, the product of science. [...] When we indigenize we are fitting the entity into a pre-existing mould. Hence it would be more accurate to speak of

the autonomous development of the social sciences rather than the indigenization of the social sciences. We can adopt new cultural objects without indigenizing the object and the social sciences responsible for its creation. (Alatas 2002: 155)

I would like to avoid and reject the notion of indigenization as opposed to autonomous development of sociology, or any science for that matter. Indigenization has a different connotation. In principle, a science cannot be indigenized. Only its application can. [...] Its characteristic is to break away from the indigenous tradition mould. Science is autonomous from the traditional cultural background. Every great scientific breakthrough is a rupture with the previous outlook on the subject in question. Take arithmetic: the statement that 2 + 2 = 4 cannot be indigenized. We can indigenize the script and the numeral system but not the concept. The concept has an independent existence and growth in our mind. It does not possess a concrete existence by itself. (Alatas 2006: 10)

In both excerpts, we can see that S. H. Alatas' argument bears similarities to the criticisms of indigenous sociology previously laid out in this chapter. On the one hand, S. H. Alatas endorses the view that 'indigenous sociology' is really just the indigenization of Eurocentric concepts and sociological problems – as we discussed in the case of Akiwowo's work regarding agency and *Asuwada* epistemology. Like Burawoy (2010) and Go (2016b), S. H. Alatas also highlights how 'indigenous sociology' does not make complete sense because there are some central, albeit broad and abstract, universals to sociology that apply to the discipline regardless of its area of geopolitical production (e.g. that sociology ought to study social processes, that sociology aims to explore social phenomena and so on).

However, the extent to which S. H. Alatas' alternative concept of 'autonomous sociology' differs from the notion of indigenous sociology – beyond syntax – is debatable. Just as with the turn to indigenous sociology, the call for autonomous sociology starts from the social problem of intellectual imperialism, where 'much of social science [is] assimilated uncritically outside of their countries of origin, among students, lecturers, researchers and planners' (Gamage 2018: 87). This 'uncritical assimilation', according to S. H. Alatas (2002: 152), has led to a situation whereby sociologists in the Global South are merely mimicking theories imported from the North:

> Although there are studies that are sufficiently factually oriented towards the country [...] they fail to identify significant problems pertaining to the country or region. If it is an economic study of the Philippines, it resembles many economic studies of the United States with the only difference that the facts are from the Philippines – the same method, the same concepts and the same kind of problems. I am not saying that entire Asian social science literature is of this kind. There are some good studies too, but the overriding trend is of the imitative type.

By contrast, an autonomous sociology – according to S. H. Alatas (2002) – attempts to epistemologically break from Northern theories, and to creatively develop new explanations and frameworks for the study of 'non-Western' social problems. As S. H. Alatas (2002: 150) thus highlights: 'an autonomous tradition cannot develop without the commitment of an intellectual, creative and independent group striving for that tradition'. Alatas (2006: 37) argues that this tradition of autonomous sociology will be 'defined as one which raises a problem, creates concepts and creatively applies theories in an independent manner and without being dominated intellectually by another tradition'. Creativity in thought and connecting with non-Western thought thus become defining characteristics of autonomous sociology.

Just like the approach of indigenizing sociology, therefore, S. H. Alatas' call for forming autonomous sociological traditions involves the process of looking inward to address non-Western societies. Developing this argument, S. F. Alatas (2010) argues that thinking local enables us to create theories and concepts that would not develop in the West because they escape the Western standpoint. S. F. Alatas' (2010) own example is the theory of 'colonial capitalism', a form of capitalism that is discrete from the capitalism that developed in the Western metropoles. Drawing on Rizal's (2019 [1890]) work in the Philippines, and S. H. Alatas' (2013 [1977]) work in Malaysia, S. F. Alatas (2010) argues that in colonial capitalism the social structure is maintained through the ideology of laziness and idleness, an ideology that is projected onto and towards the native populations within these societies by the colonialists. In both cases, the ideology that the natives were 'lazy' allowed the colonialists to justify seizing tenure of the natives' land.[11] Such an ideology of idleness, however, was not used as a land-seizing tactic within the metropoles. S. F. Alatas thus argues that the concept of 'idleness', as well as the theory of colonial capitalism, are two insights that an autonomous sociology can give us once it breaks with Northern theory and starts to look inwards to its own society. To study the Philippines and Malaysia solely through Northern theory, such as the capitalist theory developed by Karl Marx, S. F. Alatas argues, obfuscates the actual ideological and material processes and structures within these societies.[12]

However, just as with the indigenous sociology approach, we can question the extent to which even the notion of 'autonomous sociology' succeeds in decentring the hegemony of Western sociology. As S. F. Alatas (2000, 2006) argues, sculpting an autonomous sociology does not necessitate an outright rejection of any sociology coming from the West. Rather, the issue is to avoid uncritical mimicry; a tradition of autonomous sociology allows for the sociologists in question to import Western social science, so long as they have good reason to do so. If Western theory critically 'works', according to S. F. Alatas (2000), then in this situation there is no problem with it being imported to a non-Western scenario. In this line of thought, Bhambra (2014) has highlighted how autonomous sociology essentially involves the 'strategic' importing of Western theory. Further, this is precisely where the problem of an 'autonomous sociology' lies: almost all of S. F. Alatas' discussion about autonomous social science revolves around comparing 'regional' socio-logical traditions (e.g. the 'Asian tradition') with the Western tradition. In doing so, much of Alatas' intellectual energy is spent discussing when it is appropriate to import Western theory and when it is more appropriate to instead connect with one's regional tradition. What is lost, therefore, is a discussion of when to engage with *other* non-Western 'tradi-tions' of sociology, if at all. This speaks to the wider problem of well-meaning sociologists and institutions highlighting different national traditions of sociology – such as with the recent Palgrave 'Sociology Transformed' series highlighting sociological traditions of China (Chen 2018), Israel (Ram 2018), New Zealand (Crothers 2018), Australia (Harley and Wickham 2014) and Brazil (Cordeiro and Neri 2019) – without paying attention to the conversations *between* these traditions, aside from their united rejection of Eurocentrism. As Bhambra (2014: 94) thus points out, the concept of an autonomous sociology ends up with a set of different regional sociologies, all remaining discrete from one another, orbiting around the West:

> The model of global sociology being posited here is of creative, autonomous, regional satellites orbiting the West where all the satellites need to refer to the West but it has no requirement to refer to them, or they to each other.

The notion of autonomous sociologies, rather than displacing Western sociological hegemony, ends up recen-tring this very same episteme. Autonomous sociology ends up becoming a project discussing 'Which bits of Western theory shall we apply to our society?' rather than 'What can we learn from other sociological traditions?' The West remains the centre that the rest of the world can learn from, while the other modes of thought are precisely that – the 'other' to the norm.

Autonomous and indigenous sociology: Calls to build autonomous or indigenous sociologies start from the premise that sociologists in the South need to reject intellectual imperialism, and build their own systems of sociological thought. Scholars such as Akinsola Akiwowo (1986, 1999) thus argue that 'indigenous' sociologies should explore local problems through local epistemologies – as he does in using the *Asuwada* epistemology coming from the Yoruban oral tradition. Other scholars, such as Syed Farid Alatas (2010), argue that we need to build 'autonomous' sociologies which connect with regional traditions (such as the tradition of 'Asian sociology'), and ought to reject the uncritical mimicry of Western theory in non-Western contexts.

From the 'what' back to the 'why'

Both the calls for indigenizing sociology and those for creating autonomous sociologies, therefore, face problems in decentring Western sociology. However, perhaps we ought not to be concerned with whether or not either of these projects has 'succeeded' in its aims, and instead praise them for the counter-narrative of sociology that they provide.[13] The calls for building autonomous and indigenous sociologies do not stem from a desire to merely create national or local paradigms of social thought. These calls stem from a desire to challenge the intellectual imperialism maintained in sociology. In challenging this intellectual imperialism, those calling for autonomous and indigenous sociologies thus raise important questions concerning canonization in sociology. As Alatas and Sinha (2001) discuss in the context of Singapore, why should sociology students be required to read thinkers such as Marx and Weber who generalized 'the East' as pre-modern? More generally, why should students across the Global South be encouraged to value a sociological canon that has either ignored or Orientalized their cultures? These questions speak to wider issues of valuation.

Building autonomous or indigenous sociological models is part of a wider project of the struggle for dignity, respect and recognition, coming from a range of diverse people who have all been devalued through colonial difference. Valuing the subjectivities of these people necessitates valuing their epistemologies too. The problem, as captured by Santos (2014: 1), is that Western sociology does not provide this valuation to either these subjectivities or these epistemologies, creating a situation whereby 'We know Marx, even though Marx may not know us.' By contrast to Marx, there is an infinite list of intellectuals producing sociological knowledge who *do* know us:

> We know Fanon, and Fanon knows us. We know Toussaint L'Ouverture and Toussaint L'Ouverture knows us. We know Patrice Lumumba, and Patrice Lumumba knows us. We know Bartolina Sisa, and Bartolina Sisa knows us. We know Catarina Eufémia, and Catarina Eufémia knows us. We know Rosa Parks, and Rosa Parks knows us. But *the large majority of those who know us are not well known*. We are revolutionaries with no papers. (Santos 2014: 1, emphasis added)

In order to decolonize sociology, therefore, we can learn effective lessons from the calls to indigenize or autonomize sociology. On the one hand, we have the issue of those theorists who do *not* 'know us'. How do we build links with these scholars that neglected the subaltern? How do we, so to speak, allow Marx to 'know us'? On the other hand, there is the issue of those scholars who know us but 'are not well known'. What happens to our wider understanding of sociology once we value the social thought of these intellectuals? How can putting these disparate intellectuals into dialogue with one another enrich our sociological understandings? These are questions we now turn to when discussing critical thinkers building conversational sociologies.

Further reading

Articles

Alatas, Syed Farid. 2003. 'Academic Dependency and the Global Division of Labour in the Social Sciences'. *Current Sociology* 51 (6): 599–613.
Syed Farid Alatas' paper sketches out his theory of intellectual imperialism. In this paper, Alatas thus shows the similarities between economic dependency and academic dependency, and theorizes control over knowledge production as being a key facet of contemporary imperial relations.

Connell, Raewyn, Fran Collyer, João Maia and Robert Morrell. 2017. 'Toward a Global Sociology of Knowledge: Post-Colonial Realities and Intellectual Practices'. *International Sociology* 32 (1): 21–37.
Raewyn Connell, Fran Collyer, João Maia and Robert Morrell use this paper to discuss the sociology of knowledge production on a global scale. Drawing on empirical case studies of intellectuals in Australia, South Africa and Brazil, the authors show that Northern theory and institutions remain hegemonic in the global political economy of knowledge, and that Southern intellectuals must thus adopt a range of extraverted strategies – including knowing where to publish, how to frame their research and who to collaborate with – in order to persevere in the academic world.

Onwuzuruigbo, Ifeanyi. 2018. 'Indigenising Eurocentric Sociology: The "Captive Mind" and Five Decades of Sociology in Nigeria'. *Current Sociology* 66 (6): 831–48.
Ifeanyi Onwuzuruigbo's paper looks specifically at sociology in Nigeria. Onwuzuruigbo examines how sociology in Nigeria has been shaped by Eurocentric intellectual imperialism, while also paying attention to the various attempts to indigenize sociology in response to this imperialism.

Books

Bhambra, Gurminder K. 2014. *Connected Sociologies*. London: Bloomsbury.

Gurminder Bhambra's book firstly analyses how traditional Eurocentric sociology has largely analysed Western society, and the processes of Western modernity, outside of its relations with coloniality. Bhambra thus sketches out the various attempts to indigenize and autonomize sociology, while demonstrating how these debates have ended up recentring Eurocentrism. By contrast, Bhambra argues that we need to move towards a practice of connected sociologies, which puts relationism at the heart of our sociological imaginations.

Patel, Sujata, ed. 2010. *The ISA Handbook of Diverse Sociological Traditions*. Los Angeles, CA: SAGE.

Sujata Patel's edited book includes many papers that highlight different regional traditions of sociology. Moreover, this edited book also highlights connections between these different sociological traditions, as well as more theoretical reflections on what it means to sculpt a 'global sociology'.

–3–

Walking While Asking Questions: Towards a 'Sociology in Conversations'

In the previous two chapters we have highlighted two problems involved in decolonizing sociology. Firstly, we have a dominant canon that is characterized by a Eurocentric standpoint. Secondly, this canon is exported across the world as being *the* universal sociological canon. Nevertheless, in the previous two chapters we have also considered the 'other side' to sociology. Thus, we considered how, while sociology may embody a Eurocentric standpoint, there are also multiple sociological paradigms that embody and work towards a Southern standpoint. Furthermore, while we considered how sociology is incorporated into the overall workings of intellectual imperialism, we also highlighted attempts within the discipline to challenge such imperialism – as seen through the indigenizing approach and calls to build autonomous traditions of sociology. In a way, therefore, I have been slightly hypocritical in my review of sociology. Namely, so far this book has given a bifurcated view of sociology: a sociology that is Eurocentric and involved in intellectual imperialism, versus a sociology embracing a Southern standpoint which is attempting to generate autonomous and/or indigenous traditions and knowledge.

However, if decolonial sociology is to be a *relational* sociology, then we need to avoid this bifurcated view of sociology and instead look to the conversations between the apparently opposite sides of the sociological coin. While is it essential to highlight the provincial nature of sociology embracing the Eurocentric standpoint, and while it is equally essential to highlight the attempts to ground approaches built from a Southern standpoint, it is also a disservice to decolonial sociology to avoid the links between different sociological traditions that have resulted in critical paradigms of social thought.

It is in this line of thought that this chapter seeks to show how a decolonial sociology is a 'sociology in conversations'. This notion of a conversational sociology takes inspiration from the Zapatista motto of 'walking while asking questions', an epistemic ethic that transcends the Western commitment to 'walking while preaching' (Grosfoguel 2017: 159). This style of sociology that walks while asking questions is a sociology that does not make a claim to full universalism, but looks to realize and address its blind spots through putting itself into conversations with alternative frameworks, lived experiences and social realities. Through putting itself into such conversations, this sociology is built on the epistemic principle that we ought to ultimately work together – between frameworks, traditions, concepts and so on – to achieve the most critical paradigms of social thought. Some have labelled this epistemological approach 'pluriversality'.

Pluriversality starts from the premise that no individual system of social thought – whether that be Marxist, Weberian or Khaldūnian – is complete. Rather than internalizing a vertical hierarchy between different system of thought, pluriversality in sociology involves 'a horizontal strategy of openness to dialogue among different epistemic traditions' (Mbembe 2016: 37). Before the term 'pluriversal' was even coined, decolonial scholars were already discussing social reality and the formation of knowledge in this way. For instance, Césaire discussed the notion of a universal knowledge constituted by multiple particulars, that is 'a universal rich with all that is particular, rich with all particulars, the deepening and coexistence of all particulars' (Grosfoguel 2017: 155). Such an approach by Césaire thus laid the groundwork for a theory of pluriversality as he theorized universalism not in the sense of one, consistent, overarching theory used to explain all social reality, but rather as being 'the result of a horizontal process of critical dialogue between peoples who relate to one another as equals' (Grosfoguel 2017: 156).

In parallel with Césaire's approach, a pluriversal sociology is a sociology involved in a horizontal dialogue between *sociologies* which relate to one another as equals. To quote Mignolo (2007: 500), crafting this horizontal sociology thus becomes 'quite demanding. It demands, basically, that we cannot have it all our own way.' No sociology can 'have it all [its] own way' because a critical sociology is in fact composed of *multiple* sociologies interacting with one another – what Bhambra (2014) terms 'connected sociologies'. This chapter discusses instances of this 'connected', pluriversal sociology in action.

On your Marx

The works of Marx are perhaps one of the greatest examples for how a decolonial sociology does not necessitate a dismantling of 'Northern theory', but rather involves a horizontal, reflexive, conversational approach. One exercise, for instance, that I do in the classroom for my course on racialized capitalism is to ask my class to name famous Marxists from the twentieth century with whom they are familiar. Due to the way that theory is taught at our university and elsewhere, you will get names like Adorno, Horkheimer, Marcuse and the school of critical theory floating around. However, other names also come to the students' minds, such as W. E. B. Du Bois, C. L. R James, Aimé Césaire, Amílcar Cabral, Fanon, Claudia Jones, Angela Davis, Cedric Robinson, Rosa Luxemburg and Stuart Hall.[1] Implicit in the classroom's understanding is that the people who were breathing life into

Marxism throughout the twentieth century, and scholars from whom we are still taking inspiration, were anti-colonial or anti-imperialist thinkers who were committed to global and relational analysis. All of these thinkers thought *against* Marxism, but also *with* Marxism. Further, they did not think with Marxism in virtue of intellectual imperialism, but because they put their realities and topics of investigation into dialogue with the theories they judged to be capable of critical analysis. Moreover, in many of the cases, these thinkers who have been seen as pioneers of decolonial sociology developed their critical Marxisms through their travels and interactions *within* the metropoles, once again highlighting that movement and transnational conversation are essential components of decolonial sociology. While we have considered how classical Marxism may fall into the trap of Orientalism and bifurcation, we thus equally need to focus on those thinkers who developed their own strand of decolonial Marxism.

Decolonial Marxism: Decolonial Marxism refers to the programme of analysing colonialism, empire and imperialism through a Marxist lens. However, decolonial Marxism works both with and against classical Marxism. It works *with* classical Marxism by giving primary importance to studying the base and economic relations of society (and societies), and by viewing the logic of capital accumulation as a key driver in the modern world. It works *against* – or, in Fanon's (1963 [1961]) word, 'stretches' – classical Marxism in virtue of analysing how the logic of capital accumulation was also a driving force of colonialism and imperialism. Additionally going against classical Marxism, decolonial Marxism looks at how the colonized and enslaved became a class apart from the proletariat, and how a global white, Western proletariat thus joined with the bourgeoisie in exploiting this subalternized group.

Du Bois and racialized capitalism

Take, for instance, the sociology of W. E. B. Du Bois – a 'forgotten scholar' who is currently being rewritten into the history of sociology across Western universities.[2] Some of Du Bois' earlier known sociological contributions centre on his work as director of the Atlanta Sociological Laboratory, founded in 1896, thus becoming the first empirical school of sociology in the US (Wright 2002a). Du Bois' work at the Atlanta School in the late nineteenth and early twentieth centuries focused on the empirical investigation of social problems facing Black people in the US's new urban inner cities.[3]

However, outside of his work at Atlanta, Du Bois also had a globally oriented sociology which simultaneously took aim at the transnational nature of racialization and at how this global racialization shaped the world order.[4] In *Dusk of Dawn*, Du Bois (2007 [1940]) thus states that his *global* interest in race was sparked by his travels across European metropoles, encompassing London, Berlin, Paris and Brussels among other cities.[5] As Du Bois recounts, he therefore began his trajectory by seeing the situation of US Black folk as being incredibly particular to the US, before expanding his conceptual horizon across the entire globe ruled by 'white Europe':

> For long years it seemed to me that this imprisonment of a human group with chains in hands of an environing group, was a singularly unusual characteristic of the Negro in the United States in the nineteenth century. But since then it has been easy for me to realize that the majority of mankind has struggled through this inner spiritual slavery and that while a dream which we have easily and jauntily called democracy envisages a day when the environing group looses the chains and compulsion, and is willing and even eager to grant families, nations, sub-races, and races equality of opportunity among larger groups, that even

this grand equality has not come; and until it does, individual equality and the free soul is impossible. All our present frustration in trying to realize individual equality through communism, fascism, and democracy arises from our continual unwillingness to break the intellectual bonds of group and racial exclusiveness. [...] Thus it is impossible for the clear-headed student of human action in the United States and *in the world*, to avoid facing the fact of a white world which is today dominating human culture and working for the continued subordination of the colored races. (Du Bois 2007 [1940]: 69–70, emphasis added)

Thus, it is quite clear that Du Bois (2008 [1920]: 308) appreciated the *global* nature of racialization, as articulated in his description of the world system where 'Everything great, good, efficient, fair and honorable is "white". Everything mean, bad, blundering, cheating and dishonorable is "yellow", brown and black.'[6] Indeed, Du Bois' often-quoted line about the problem of the twentieth century being the problem of the colour line tends to also occlude the fact that he was talking about a *global* colour line, speaking to the relations between 'the darker to the lighter races of men in Asia and Africa, in America and the islands of the sea' (Du Bois 2007 [1903]: 15).[7]

Precisely how Du Bois then analysed this global racial hierarchy was through a *Marxist framework*. As Du Bois (2007 [1940]: 151) himself recalled, he saw great value in the works of Marx in that:

I believed and still believe that Karl Marx was one of the greatest men of modern times and that he put his finger squarely upon our difficulties when he said that economic foundations, the way in which men earn their living, are the determining factors in the development of civilization, in literature, religion, and the basic pattern of culture. And this conviction I had to express or spiritually die.

However, as per the ethos of this chapter, Du Bois thought both *with* and *against* Marx, in a way that therefore expanded the scope of Marxist theory through a Southern standpoint. In particular, Du Bois reconfigured Marxist theory to account for the wider presence of coloniality, paying specific attention to the relations between different national iterations of capitalism across the world.

Take for instance Du Bois' (2014 [1935]) *Black Reconstruction*. In this book he analyses how the US's cotton production – fuelled by the labour of the enslaved – created an economic revolution in the US, particularly creating 'new miracles for manufacturing, and particularly for the spinning and weaving of cloth' (Du Bois 2014 [1935]: 56). However, the US was not just producing cotton for its own internal market; rather, cotton was a key trading resource in the wider global economy. In fact, a lot of this cotton produced by the enslaved was exported to the United Kingdom, and was then spun in the British factories and exported on to India and other colonies.[8] Through exporting these materials to India, Britain was simultaneously able to supress the Indian cotton industry, which, prior to colonial rule, was the dominant textile market in the global economy (Bhambra 2010). This is a perfect demonstration of why Gilroy (1993) encourages us to think of 'the boat' in Du Boisian thought – in the sense of needing to analyse the travels and routes of racialized capital and labour across the globe – given that, as Du Bois (2014 [1935]: 56–7) comments:

> Black labor became the foundation stone not only of the Southern social structure, but of Northern manufacture and commerce, of the English factory system, of European commerce, of buying and selling on a world-wide scale.

Du Bois thus retained the Marxist focus on exploitation and capital, but widened the scope to tease out colonial and imperial relations. To Du Bois (2007 [1940]: 96), global capitalism itself was a system based on 'the domination of white Europe over black Africa and yellow Asia, through political power built on the economic control of labor, income and ideas'. This is a patently Marxist interpretation of capitalism which directs the analysis towards the economic base and relations of production of a given system; however, this theory extends the Marxist focus to account for how these *relations of production were colonial and imperial relations*. Du Bois argues that through this global political economy that is based on exploiting the colonialized and enslaved, the colonized people become a 'class below' the traditional Marxist definition of the worker – on both a national and a global scale. For instance, within the US, Du Bois (2014 [1935]: 205) points out how classical Marxist theory struggles to cope once we put imperial relations in the centre of our analysis, given that 'the workers' are themselves bifurcated along racialized lines; to Du Bois, Marxism:

> did not envisage a situation where instead of a horizontal division of classes, there was a vertical fissure, a complete separation of classes by race, cutting square across the economic layers [...] and this split depended not simply on economic exploitation but on a racial folk-lore grounded on centuries of instinct, habit and thought and implemented by the conditioned reflex of visible color.

Through the concept that later became termed the 'wages of whiteness', Du Bois thus referenced how across the US and Europe, white workers were still awarded some benefit through the relations of global capitalism.[9]

Such a racialization of global capitalism – through imperialism, colonialism and enslavement – thus created a 'class stratification *within* the working class' (Magubane 2000: 344; emphasis added). Indeed, Du Bois (2014 [1935]: 99) points out that abolitionist movements in places such as the United Kingdom were already starting from this recognition that it was not just a white bourgeoisie but also white workers who were contributing to the exploitation of the enslaved and colonized, as captured in a letter written to the US by the English George Holyoake in 1857, signed by 1,800

English workers, where they argued that 'the black worker was furnishing the raw material which the English capitalist was exploiting together with the English worker'. While Du Bois thus maintained a Marxist ethos in studying the material base of society and the relationship between capital and labour in the capitalist mode of production, his transnational focus allowed him to look at divisions of labour and capital *within* the proletariat itself, and how the system of global capitalism was actually built on the foundations of colonial exploitation and expropriation, and enslaved labour. In other words, he *stretched* the epistemic and empirical boundaries of Marxism by constructing a relational framework of transnational connections.

Fanon, Shari'ati and capitalism: widening the Marxist scope

Du Bois' analysis of how the white worker and bourgeoisie alike benefited from colonialism and enslavement was a route of thought taken by theorists of racial capitalism. Famously, Roediger (2017) built upon Du Bois' work to theorize the 'wages of whiteness' in capitalism – the process through which white workers acquire a specific psychological and economic 'wage' over Black and brown workers. One of Roediger's arguments is that in virtue of being racialized as white, white workers in the US practise racism and see themselves as more valuable than their Black counterparts *as a specific way of dealing with their own alienation in capitalist society.*[10] However, this consequence of alienation, whereby white workers come to 'side' with their racialized rather than classed membership, does not seem to be systemically theorized in classical Marxism despite the centrality of the concept of alienation to this paradigm of social thought. The extent to which classical Marxism sufficiently analysed the concept of alienation, *outside of the confines of a de-racialized working class versus a de-racialized bourgeoisie,* can therefore be called into question.

Fanon was one theorist who thought with and against Marx in order to expand the concept of alienation to account for its use in colonialism. In doing so, Fanon exposed how classical Marxist theory was guilty of the false universalism typical of the colonial episteme that we criticized in this book's earlier chapters. As Fanon shows us, Marx may have critically analysed the alienation of workers in the West, but because alienation works differently in different places and towards different people, there is a significant problem with going from this provincial case to a universal theory of capitalist alienation.

Consider, therefore, the classical Marxist account of alienation. In his 1844 *Economic and Philosophic Manuscripts*, Marx (2007 [1932]) argues that there are four types of alienation typical of workers in capitalism:

1. *Alienation from product*: This form of alienation speaks to the division of labour in capitalism. In a capitalist system, that which is produced by the worker(s) is owned by the capitalist. In this regard, the worker loses identification with the product of their work.
2. *Alienation from productive activity*: Given that what the workers produce is owned by the capitalist, and that in a sense the capitalist 'owns' the labourer, workers lose their ability to affirm themselves through their work. Instead, workers only feel themselves outside of work, and the worker's purpose in life becomes nothing more than meeting material needs.
3. *Alienation from species*: Marx argues that unlike animals, humans are a 'conscious being'. Through the monotonous nature of capitalist production, workers get converted into physical beings – akin to animals.
4. *Alienation from other humans*: Capitalism transforms human relations into economic relations, meaning that social life in general becomes competitive.

One can see quite quickly that this account of alienation in capitalism seems to be based on the case of white workers across Europe. Once we put this theory of capitalism and alienation *into conversation* with processes of colonialism and imperialism, we see that not only do some of these forms of alienation – from species and other humans, for instance

– acquire a different meaning, but also there are *additional forms of alienation not captured in classical Marxism*. Fanon is one scholar who enables us to open up the theory of alienation as such.

'"Look, a Negro!"', Fanon (2008 [1952]: 82) begins a chapter of *Black Skin, White Masks*, continuing:

> I came into the world imbued with the will to find a meaning in things, my spirit filled with the desire to attain to the source of the world, and then *I found that I was an object in the midst of other objects*.

What Fanon is describing in this quote is the nature of racialization in colonialism. The only people who were able to racialize themselves were white, while colonized others became *objects* of racialization rather than being construed as human subjects. Indeed, it is through this viewpoint that Fanon points out the exclusionary nature of Western humanism: through racializing themselves as white, Western people ascribed themselves full humanity. By contrast, the colonized *others* were all racialized as sub-human, and thus denied human rights and protections. Fanon (2008 [1952]: 3) thus argued that it was through the practices of colonial racial violence that white Europeans could constantly reaffirm their status as being full humans, captured in his quote that 'The white man slaves to reach a human level.' However, as per the decolonial spirit of *relational* analysis, Fanon thus points out that the dominant racial group relies on the existence of the Other in order to retain their status as fully human: that is, whites could not define themselves as fully human without contrasting themselves with racialized sub-humans. Of interest to Fanon was how those racialized as Black and sub-human then became aware of the racial myths produced by white colonizers. It is in this study of the psychology of colonial racism that we see Fanon produce an alternative account of alienation from what we see in classical Marxism.

In Fanon's understanding of alienation, we begin not with the economic relation between the bourgeoisie and worker, but rather with the *racialized ontological relation* between the colonizer and colonized. Fanon thus points out that while the white 'masters' require the existence of a subordinate to maintain their superiority, the colonized subordinates strive for these masters to recognize them as equals. Fanon (2008 [1952]: 3) argues that this relationship highlights the psychological violence of colonialism, whereby we see a form of internalized oppression on behalf of the colonized, captured in his statement that:

> The white man is sealed in his whiteness. The black man in his blackness. [...] White men consider themselves superior to black men. [...] Black men want to prove to white men, at all costs, the richness of their thought, the equal value of their intellect.

By focusing on this psychological violence of colonialism, Fanon's theory of alienation thus analyses the process of internalized oppression, or what Hall (1996: 446) describes as 'the internalization of the self-as-other'. Fanon's argument is that colonialism alienates Black people from themselves, because such colonized people become constantly aware of being watched, judged, stigmatized and excluded by the dominant social group. As Fanon (2008 [1952]: 87) describes:

> I move slowly in the world, accustomed now to seek no longer for upheaval. I progress by crawling. And already I am being dissected under white eyes, the only real eyes. I am *fixed*. Having adjusted their microtomes, they objectively cut away slices of my reality. I am laid bare. I feel, I see in those white faces that it is not a new man who has come in, but a new kind of man, a new genus. Why, it's a Negro!

Through investigating this process of Black, colonized people 'being dissected under white eyes', Fanon thus brings new meanings to classical Marxist approaches to alienation. Consider, for instance, the Marxian focus on alienation from species, and alienation from other humans. In colonialism, you are alienated from your species-being not just in virtue of the labour you are forced into, but also in virtue of being considered a sub-species. Fanon (2008 [1952]: 2) refers to this dimension of colonial alienation through the concept of the 'zone of non-being' – an ontological space where Black colonized people exist as a sub-species, but are not seen to exist as humans.[11] Similarly, in the colonial encounter you are alienated from other humans not just in virtue of the class relations and competition that are born through capitalism, but also because the 'myth' of race dictates that differently racialized people are inherently different from one another. While Marx may have argued, therefore, that (white, Western) workers do not 'feel themselves' at work due to monotonous capitalist production, Fanon shows that the colonized can *never* feel like themselves, as their whole schemes of self-recognition and valuation were ruptured by the material and psychological violence of colonialism.

Zone of non-being: Fanon uses the concept of the zone of non-being to speak about the dehumanization of those racialized as Black in colonialism. Within the zone of non-being, the colonized are associated with primitiveness and likened to animals, with this dehumanization justifying acts of extreme violence towards the colonized; thus Lewis Gordon (2007) refers to the zone of non-being as 'hell on earth'. The zone of non-being is thus invoked by Fanon to describe both the physical acts of brutality directed towards the colonized, and the symbolic violence of denying the colonized an autonomous sense of being.

Nevertheless, Fanon's analysis of alienation is not wholly opposed to the Marxist critique of capitalism. Rather, as he wrote in *The Wretched of the Earth*, Fanon (1963 [1961]: 40) argued that 'Marxist analysis should always be slightly stretched every time we have to deal with the colonial problem.' Through stretching this Marxist analysis to deal with colonialism, as Fanon did, we can maintain an understanding of how colonial alienation was an essential dimension for reproducing global capitalism. Colonialism and enslavement could not have happened without the ontological denial of humanity to certain people – it was precisely through an alienation from 'being' human that those racialized as Black became interpellated into the world capitalist system through enslavement. Again, these forms of alienation in colonialism and enslavement appear different – in terms of the material and ontological consequences – from what we see in the classical Marxist account of white workers' alienation in the West. However, this limitation is only a problem in a *bifurcated* sociology. A conversational sociology – as we have seen with Fanon – enables us to revise, stretch and critically develop paradigms of social thought. It is in this spirit that it becomes useful not only to put Marx into conversation with Fanon, but to add another seat at the table and introduce the works of Ali Shari'ati.

While Fanon is a key anti-colonial thinker, we must not forget that he travelled to and worked in the metropole of Paris in the mid-twentieth century. It was in this imperial metropole that Fanon encountered both neo-Marxists and existentialists such as Jean-Paul Sartre – whose work he both influenced and was influenced by.[12] Another anti-colonial thinker who was based in Paris at a similar time to Fanon was the Iranian intellectual Ali Shari'ati. Just like Fanon, Shari'ati encountered neo-Marxists and existentialists while in Paris, but Shari'ati and Fanon were also in conversation with one another – both by mail and in person – with Shari'ati also translating many of Fanon's works into Persian for other Iranian intellectuals.[13] While Shari'ati and Fanon disagreed over the role of religion in anti-colonial struggle, with Shari'ati seeing religion as potentially emancipatory and Fanon seeing it as a slippery slope into elitist autocracy, they both started from a similar frame of reference. Namely, both thinkers argued that the colonial or imperial imposition of capitalism from the West requires a *destruction* of the colony's history. This is captured in Fanon's (1963 [1961]: 209) often-quoted:

colonialism is not simply content to impose its rule upon the present and the future of a dominated country. Colonialism is not satisfied merely with holding a people in its grip and emptying the native's brain of all form and content. By a kind of perverted logic, it turns to the past of the oppressed people, and distorts, disfigures, and destroys it.

To Fanon, this destruction and devaluation of history happens through the racialization of the world system, where Blackness in particular is relegated to the zone of non-being. On the other hand, to Shari'ati (1986), who was writing from the case of Western imperialism in Iran, this destruction of history functioned through a distortion of religious values. Thus, Shari'ati criticized how Western imperialism in Iran and the surrounding areas distorted the true message of Islam, meaning that the elite – most of whom were educated in the metropoles – pursued a life of Western secularism, while the revolutionaries were marred by an uncritical religious fanaticism.

Given that Shari'ati was interested in the role of religion (and specifically Islam) in the fight for social justice, he maintained a reflexive relation to Marxism. On the one hand, Shari'ati (1980) positioned himself against Marxism and theories such as Leninism, both of which were said to only analyse religion as something that is used by the capitalist class to reproduce inequality.[14] However, just as with Du Bois and Fanon, Shari'ati goes *against* and *through* classical Marxist theory in order to stretch the critical scope of the theory in general. Indeed, there is a parallel between the way that Shari'ati complicates Marxism and the way that Fanon does. Both Fanon and Shari'ati complicate the classical Marxist divide between the base and the super-structure of society. Put simply, to Marx (2004 [1867]), the base of a society (its material relations) give rise to the super-structure (its ideas and institutions). Both Fanon and Shari'ati, on the other hand, reconfigured what exactly we should 'place' in the base of society in our analysis. Fanon (1963 [1961]: 39), for instance, argued that racialization becomes articulated into the base of society when he says that:

In the colonies the economic substructure is also a superstructure. The cause is the consequence; you are rich because you are white, you are white because you are rich.

By similar logic, Shari'ati places religion in the base of society too. In fact, Shari'ati (1986) argues that while classical Marxism wants to construe religion as something superstructural, it actually shows something quite different in its analysis. Namely, Shari'ati argues that through contending that religion is an 'opiate of the people' – that is, an ideology that allows for comfort in the face of exploitation – Marxism actually shows that religion itself has a *causal* dimension that itself inspires actions and beliefs, and ought to thus be placed in the base of society. As Shari'ati (1986: 42) puts it:

> pseudo-intellectuals, like traditionalists, view materialism/spiritualism or objectivity/subjectivity as two separate and independent entities. They do not understand that when they reiterate ready-made clichés such as 'religion is the opiate of the masses', they admit of a necessity that religion is not exclusively a simple superstructure – a product of the mode of production and economic relations of a society. Rather, it is the base and the first cause of everything. In other words, they have attributed a causal role to religion, a role which enables it to find its way into the economic infrastructure of society.

Shari'ati was thus not an anti-Marxist, but rather of the belief that classical Marxism helps us to only understand 'half of the social reality' (quoted in Zeiny 2017: 76). Thus, while criticizing how Marxism deals with the issue of religion – which Shari'ati (1980) relates to Marxism's general Eurocentrism – he uses a Marxist framework for understanding inequality in Iran and imperial inequality transnationally. Thus, in *Marxism and Other Western Fallacies*, when discussing inequality in Iran, Shari'ati (1980:

67) adopts a critique of capitalist production and its alienation of the worker in a way that runs directly parallel to Marxist thought:

> This exploitation has resulted in greater accumulations of wealth alongside more stark poverty. A peasant formerly could keep several cows, sheep, and chickens at his home to live on. He had his own small plot of land. Likewise, most implements of production, such as a mule, pick and shovel, belonged to the peasant. Thus the peasant was himself a sort of proprietor. When he became a worker, however, as he left home in the morning, he had nothing to take with him but his work clothes and a clean shave. He simply took his good right arm to the factory for eight hours and tired himself out, to collect, say twenty tumans and go home. Not being able to afford a moment's negligence, he would become daily more wedded to the machine. The peasant, on the other hand, had been a free man, working for five months out of the year and deciding himself what was to be done. He felt free. But for the worker, this sense of freedom no longer exists, nor is there a moment's leisure to think, a moment's escape from work.

Shari'ati's break from Marxism, however, stems from his answer to where the revolution comes from. To Shari'ati, the answer to this exploitation and alienation from capitalism comes not *just* from a workers' movement, but from an embracing of Shi'a Islam theology.

Through the teachings of Ali, the First Imam in Shi'a Islam, Shari'ati (1980) argues there are three dimensions of social life in which practice is needed in order to liberate the masses. Firstly, Shari'ati emphasizes the teaching and practice of the 'primacy of existence'. Here, the aim is 'to promote the existential

"I'" (Shari'ati 1980: 72), by which Shari'ati means the need to theorize one's self outside of one's position in the capitalist system (which is alienating), outside of doctrines of religious fanaticism (which denies free will), and outside of Western Marxism (where people become one-dimensional). This existentialism is based on the Shi'a principle that people are simultaneously dust (matter) and divine (embodiments of Allah's will), and that one's aim in life is to realize this divinity through free will. Secondly, Shari'ati (1980: 72) emphasizes the Shi'a teaching and practice of justice, defined as 'material justice among classes and nations, as it applies to colonization and domestic exploitation'. Here, Shari'ati counters the Orientalist depiction of Islam as anti-progress, and instead emphasizes that the entire religion was based upon the revolutionary teaching and actions of the First Prophet as he emancipated the masses from autocratic rule. Lastly, Shari'ati emphasizes the Shi'a teaching and practice of mysticism and love, meaning religion itself. Here, the emphasis is on a form of spirituality that encourages a critique of 'human alienation in a world shaped by modern economic, political, and cultural relations of domination' (Saffari 2015: 245). Shari'ati was of the belief that practice in these three dimensions of Shi'a Islam in tandem with one another is needed, and in doing so, a revolutionary ethos can be built around the Islamic principles of spirituality, equality and freedom.

The religious sociology of Shari'ati, therefore, is another example of how a decolonial, conversational sociology works.[15] Firstly, Shari'ati puts classical Marxism into conversation with Shi'a theology *and* the empirical realities of Iranian society, in a way that therefore deepens the critical capabilities of Marxism beyond its original scope. However, Shari'ati was not just in conversation with Western theory, but also took great inspiration from Fanon. As we saw,

Shari'ati's critique of Marxism had similarities to Fanon's, in the way that both theorists emphasized the need for imperial or colonial powers to destroy the history of their territories, and how race and religion respectively come into the base of capitalist society. The flow of knowledge, and the conversations being processed, therefore, are not just going from the metropoles out to the peripheries, but also *between* the peripheries themselves. Indeed, there is also knowledge from the peripheries which feeds into the metropoles – not just in terms of anti-colonial thinkers coming to places like Paris to live and work, as did Shari'ati and Fanon, but also in terms of the flows of knowledge. We can demonstrate this with a discussion of Foucault and Bourdieu.

The hidden links in Bourdieu's and Foucault's social thought

It is hard, if not impossible, to take a crash course in social theory without encountering at least one of Bourdieu or Foucault. However, what is often left out in these courses is Foucault's and Bourdieu's relations with the Global South, and how these relations are essential to the formative theories for which these authors have become canonized. Thus, we regularly teach and reproduce a bifurcated sociology which – in the case of Bourdieu and Foucault, among many others – does a disservice to how their transnational experiences and conversations shaped their canonical paradigms of thought. Part of the problem, again ironically for sociology, is that we regularly divorce theorists such as Foucault and Bourdieu from the world in which they were doing sociology. Thus, if we open up our scope from not just Bourdieu and Foucault but French social theory more generally, the canonical authors of this tradition – including Sartre, de Beauvoir, Althusser, Derrida, Lyotard, Lévi-Strauss, Bourdieu, Foucault, Leiris and Cixous – were all writing at a time in the mid-twentieth century when the French empire was rapidly losing colonies and brutally attempting to cling on to the ones it had.[16] As Nirmal Puwar (2009: 371) points out, however, despite this historical context for the emergence of French social theory, 'the colonial and post-colonial presence in the[ir] historical practice of [...] intellectual explorations has not been centred in the communication of [their] intellectual corpus in lecture theatres'. This elision of colonial and postcolonial connections is particularly apparent in the works of Bourdieu and Foucault.

Both Bourdieu and Foucault were firmly embedded in the French 'empire/knowledge complex'.[17] Upon completing military service in Algiers, Bourdieu taught at the University of Algiers from 1957 to the 1960s, while his ethnographic research on the Kabyle formed the main empirical content for his canonized works such as *The Logic of Practice* (Bourdieu 1990a) and *Outline of a Theory of Practice* (1977).[18] Similarly, Foucault taught at the University of Tunis between 1966 and 1968, ten years after Tunisian independence from France,[19] while he also travelled to Tehran at the height of the Iranian revolution in 1978, working as a reporter for the Italian newspaper *Corriere della sera*.[20] Importantly, Bourdieu and Foucault were not just working in this colonial/postcolonial world, but they were also attentive to the empirical realities of these spaces and the theorists of colonialism and imperialism. Thus, while Foucault was in Iran during the revolution against the Shah, he argued that Shari'ati's intellectual works on spiritualism formed the epistemological bedrock of the social movement, and pointed out how Iranian revolutionaries saw Shari'ati as a martyr (Foucault 2010 [1978]). Similarly, despite Edward Saïd's (1989) assertion that Bourdieu did not analyse colonialism in his works, Bourdieu and Saïd went on to invite each other to colloquia in France and the US, engaging with one another's work;[21] moreover, Bourdieu was in conversation with a host of other scholars of colonialism, in ways including a critique of Fanon's revolutionary ideas (Bourdieu 1990b), and was even chosen to write postcolonial scholar Mammeri's obituary for the French newspaper *Le Monde* in 1989 (Puwar 2009). To neglect these transnational conversations is therefore to lose a sense of the overall empirical and theoretical grounding of Foucault's and Bourdieu's works.

In the case of Bourdieu, for instance, his canonical concepts such as 'field' and 'habitus' were actually formed not just through empirical research in Algiers, but specifically through a critique of French colonialism.[22] This information, however, seems counter to the dominant approach to Bourdieu in contemporary sociology, where concepts like 'habitus' and 'field', as well as Bourdieusian sociology more generally, are mostly seen to be confined to studying social class.[23] Thus, as Go (2013b) argues, Bourdieu's (1961 [1958]) analysis of French colonialism as a system of oppression in Algeria laid the foundations for his concept of the field. Bourdieu (1961 [1958]: 120) characterized colonialism as a 'relationship of domination' that gave rise to a caste system reproduced through physically coercive racism. As Bourdieu (1961 [1958]: 146) thus clarifies, 'repression by force' – as we see in the Algerian war of independence – merely followed the logic of the colonial system, a logic which 'allows for the dominant caste to keep the dominated caste in a position of inferiority'. As Go (2013b) points out, Bourdieu's analysis of colonialism as a system involving a 'relationship of domination', and 'whose internal necessity and logic it is important to understand' (Bourdieu 1961 [1958]: 120), corresponds directly to his later fleshed-out concept of the 'field' – as a systematic set of social relations, characterized by struggles over resources, following a specific internal logic and hierarchy.[24]

Bourdieu's (1961 [1958], 1979 [1963]) critique of French colonialism laid the foundations not only for the concept of field, but also for the concept of habitus.[25] In particular, it was through Bourdieu's writings on indigenous identity and culture, torn between indigeneity and colonial imposition, that the concept of habitus arises.[26] Thus, Bourdieu and Sayad (2018 [1964]) wrote about how the logic of colonialism (i.e. the field of colonialism) produced new forms of sociability, thus creating a group of people whose culture is not fully indigenous or assimilated into the French ideal, but exists as a hybrid mixture of the two. Bourdieu (1961 [1958]: 144) argues that this causes 'a sort of double inner life' which 'is a prey to frustration and inner conflict'. In such analysis, we firstly see Bourdieu hinting towards what he later termed the concept of 'habitus' – that is, sets of dispositions people acquire relative to their objective position in society (Bourdieu 1990a). However, more specifically, we see Bourdieu articulating the concept of habitus clivé (cleft habitus) that he draws out in *Sketch for a Self-Analysis* (Bourdieu 2008) and *Pascalian Meditations* (Bourdieu 2000). In these texts, Bourdieu (2008) describes his own habitus being characterized by 'internal contradictions', having grown up as a member of the French peasantry before moving into elite academia, thus creating a mismatch between objective circumstances and between the past and present, leading to a habitus 'torn by contradiction and internal division' (Bourdieu 2000: 16). Indeed, Bourdieu (Bourdieu and Passeron 1990) is perhaps best known for invoking the concept of habitus clivé when discussing social class and education in France, examining the mismatch between the lower class's educational aspirations and the objective structure of the French educational system. While Bourdieu did, therefore, invoke the concept of habitus clivé to analyse social class, we see how it is absolutely necessary to tie this concept – just as with the concept of field – back to its foundation in the empirical realities of colonialism.

Through Bourdieu's concepts of field and habitus, therefore, what we see is a reversal of the extraversion or intellectual imperialism that we have analysed in the previous chapters of this book. The theoretical concepts are constructed in the South and used to explore empirical features of Western society. Bourdieu's sociology was both conversational and transnational. Through teaching this sociology in a bifurcated way – for example, by looking at the concept of habitus in terms of class and distinction in France (Bourdieu 2010 [1979]), rather than through its original application in studying colonial cultural hybridity in Algiers – we slice off the foundational empirical and theoretical material of Bourdieu's oeuvre. In fact, Bourdieu's whole approach to sociology has been an anti-scholasticism, where sociology is seen as a 'martial art' used to battle social injustices.[27] However, Bourdieu's original application of this 'sociology as a martial art' approach was in his study of French coloni-alism. As highlighted by Puwar (2009), Bourdieu (2008: 39–40) himself argued that he wrote his critique of French colonialism in *The Algerians* (Bourdieu 1961 [1958]) 'to tell the French, and especially people on the left, what was really going on in a country of which they often knew next to nothing'. Bourdieu's sociological concepts, and whole approach to sociology in general, therefore, are not just phenomena arising in the Global North for the study of the Global North, as we see them labelled in some critiques,[28] but are themselves instances of a transnational, *conversational* sociology that transcends a North/South binary.

Similar relations can be teased out with Foucault's work on power. Namely, we could argue that while Foucault can be accused of bifurcating between metropoles and colonies, as we examined earlier in this book when considering his theory of disciplinary power and punishment in Europe, his work still has great influence for post/decolonial theory – as seen in the way that Foucault influenced scholars such as Saïd (1979) and Bhabha (1994) among others. However, the issue is – as ever – more complex. As Medien (2019) shows, Foucault may not have explicitly mentioned it in his canonical works, but there is a clear epistemic and empirical link between his experiences in Tunisia and his later writings on power. The issue, as with Bourdieu, therefore, is that the way sociologists tend to frame Foucault splits much of his work from its anti-colonial, anti-imperial roots. Thus, Foucault's intellectual trajectory tends to be framed around a move from 'archaeology' in the 1960s, to genealogy and power in the 1970s (with the May 1968 social movements in France being a catalyst for this change), and then to 'the self' in the 1980s.[29] Through this lens, 'Foucault's radical activism and scholarship are firmly identified as having erupted from a European experience, located within the European continent', rather than from his experiences in places such as Tunisia (Medien 2019: 493). This reading of Foucault seems even more puzzling given that he even commented himself that it was not the social movements in France in May 1968 that shifted him towards analyses of power, but rather his

experiences in Tunisia in the anti-imperial social movements
of March 1968: 'It wasn't May of '68 in France that changed
me; it was March of '68, in a third-world country' (Foucault
1991 [1979]: 132).

Thus, Medien (2019) provides us with a revised reading
of Foucault that sheds light on the link between Foucault's
time in Tunisia and his overall intellectual corpus. To begin
with, Medien points out that it was in Tunisia that Foucault
began his involvement in radical (anti-imperial, anti-colonial)
activism, which he then brought back with him to Paris in
September 1968 and which inspired his interest in French
prison reform (which itself became a foundation for his book
Discipline and Punish (Foucault 2019 [1975])). Following
the 'Six Day War' in Tunisia in 1967, Foucault not only gave
his apartment to the non-arrested activists who had been
campaigning against Western imperialism and Zionism, but
also helped them to produce their pamphlets, and provided a
proportion of his wage to cover legal fees for those activists
who had been arrested by the Tunisian state (Medien 2019).
A year later, in March 1968, a week of protests and strikes
took place at the University of Tunis, demanding the release
of the activists who had been imprisoned a year earlier, and
building on the calls for an end to Western imperialism
enabled by Tunisia, an end to the Vietnam war, an end to
Israeli colonialism, and an end to Tunisia's authoritarianism
(Medien 2019). Following the arrest of activists at these
protests, not only did Foucault unsuccessfully attempt to get
the Tunisian president and French ambassador to Tunisia to
release the imprisoned activists, but also submitted to court
files on his students who had been imprisoned, although
these were rejected for use as evidence in their defence
(Medien 2019). Rather than May 1968 being a catalyst for
his path into scholar activism, therefore, Foucault actually
brought back his already existing activism, sparked in March
1968, when he returned to Paris later that year. It was this
activism that he had started in Tunisia, shocked by the 'intolerable nature of certain conditions produced by capitalism,
colonialism, and neo-colonialism' (Foucault 1991 [1979]:
137), that got Foucault interested in prison reform in France

when he set up the *Groupe d'information sur les prisons* in 1970. Given that this work on prison reform directly influenced Foucault's work on punishment, the penal state and power in his *Discipline and Punish* (2019 [1975]), there is thus a clear empirical line from his time in Tunisia to his intellectual production.

Furthermore, we can build an even stronger link between Foucault's time in Tunisia and his work on power. As Medien (2019) shows, Foucault himself admits that it is in Tunisia that he first became systematically interested in theorizing power not as a possession, but as a network of productive relations. As Foucault (1991 [1979]: 144–5) says:

> what was the meaning of that outburst of radical revolt that the Tunisian students had attempted? What was it that was being questioned everywhere? I think my answer is that the dissatisfaction came from the way in which a kind of permanent oppression in daily life was being put into effect by the state or by other institutions and oppressive groups. That which was ill-tolerated and continuously questioned, which produced that sort of discomfort, was 'power'. And not only state power, but also that which was exercised within the social body through extremely different channels, forms, and institutions. It was no longer acceptable to be 'governed' in a certain way. I mean 'governed' in an extended sense; I'm not referring just to the government of the state and the men who represent it, but also to those men who organise our daily lives by means of rules, by way of direct or indirect influences, as for instance the mass media. If I look today at my past, I recall having thought that I was working essentially on a 'genealogical' history of knowledge. But the true motivating force was really this problem of power.

It is also in this context that we see Foucault coming to an understanding of governmentality – that is, an exercise of power that functions to regulate people's actions – as he discusses being '"governed" in an extended sense [...] referring [...] to those men who organise our daily lives by means of rules, by way of direct or indirect influences, as for instance the mass media'. Thus, while this network theory of power and governmentality appears in Foucault's works in the 1970s and 1980s, including *Discipline and Punish* (2019 [1975]) and three volumes of *The History of Sexuality* (1990 [1976], 2012 [1984], 2012 [1988]), his thoughts were first formulated in the context of Tunisian anti-colonial and anti-imperial activism. Foucault, therefore, did not treat his experiences in Tunisia as something that bifurcated from his intellectual work, but drew explicit links between power and resistance in France and power and resistance in Tunisia. As Foucault (1991 [1979]: 141) exclaimed: 'I am convinced that in the end, what was really at stake also in France, and what accounted for change in so many things, was of the same nature as that experience I had come to know in Tunisia.' It was through witnessing this 'same nature' – of power and resistance – that Foucault's canonical works then arose (Medien 2019).

Just as with Bourdieu, therefore, Foucault also developed a transnational, conversational approach in his sociology. Nevertheless, the way that Foucault is presented to the sociological world usually neglects these conversational, transnational links. Finding these links and building upon them becomes a key task for decolonial sociology, as we seek to move towards a critical sociology ourselves. A final example of such a dialogical, transnational sociology can be located in Patricia Hill Collins' (2019) recent work which puts intersectionality into conversation with the coloniality of gender (Lugones 2007) approach.

Intersectionality and the coloniality of gender

In her recent work, Patricia Hill Collins (2019) puts intersectionality – a theory stemming from Black feminist thought which stresses the co-articulation of racism and sexism – into conversation with decolonial feminist theory. Rather than seeing these two approaches as disparate, Collins appreciates their diversity but envisages them as collaborative, complementary 'critical knowledge projects'. While paying attention to the specific roots of intersectionality in Black feminist thought, Collins shows us what it can learn from decolonial feminism, the ways it can work in synergy with decolonial feminism, and the epistemic and methodological similarities between the two approaches as they ground themselves as critical knowledge projects.

> **Critical knowledge projects**: Patricia Hill Collins (2019) uses the notion of critical knowledge projects to refer to epistemologies that attempt to resist dominant ways of thinking and knowing. To Collins, projects like intersectionality and decolonial feminisms are examples of critical knowledge projects, as they involve women of colour and women in the Global South resisting the epistemic inequality created by white, Western feminism.

The first connection, Collins argues, is that both intersectionality and decolonial feminism(s) seek to destabilize white, Western feminism. Indeed, it is in virtue of challenging what Collins (2019: 129) construes as the '*epistemic oppression*' and '*epistemic injustice*' of white Western feminism that both these approaches ground themselves as critical knowledge projects in virtue of engaging in '*epistemic resistance*'. Thus, Collins (2019: 104) points out that in the US, women of colour, and particularly Black women:

> were especially vocal in criticizing Western feminism's long-standing focus on the experiences of white, Western, middle-class women. [...] Bringing a racial frame into feminism challenged the false universal of whiteness as a normalizing standard that was used to explain the experiences of all women.

It is from this ethic of challenging the false universal of whiteness in feminist theory that we get the tradition of inter-sectionality in Black feminist thought in the US, from figures such as Anna Julia Cooper (1990 [1892]) and Sojourner Truth (Davis 1983) in the nineteenth century through to the contemporary day in which Collins is writing. Thus, if we consider early twentieth-century feminism in the US, one of the many issues was the way that 'women' were represented as weak and feeble. However, through intersectionality – which highlights the interplay between racism and sexism – Black feminist thinkers pointed out that this was a repre-sentation specific to *white* women, as Black women were construed as physically (abnormally) strong and hyper-sexual (see Collins 2004).

Developing this critique, Collins points out that while intersectionality thus destabilized the whiteness of feminist theory through focusing on gendered racism (and racialized sexism), decolonial feminisms also destabilized this univer-salization through focusing on the processes of colonialism and imperialism:

> Racism, *colonialism, imperialism*, and nationalism, as well as the people who were most negatively affected by those forms of domination, were not seen as being central to feminist theories of gender or sexuality. (Collins 2019: 104; emphasis added)

It is here that we see how the coloniality of gender approach (Lugones 2007) works with intersectionality to sustain a more global critique of the way that 'women' in feminist analyses have been implicitly defined as white, Western women. Central to María Lugones' (2007, 2010, 2016) coloniality of gender paradigm is the point that Europe exported its model of gender through colonialism, primarily as a way of assimilating colonized people into European standards of being (thus the connection between the coloniality of being and the coloniality of gender), and as a way of 'civilizing' the colonized people. Lugones' theory of the coloniality of gender, therefore, argues that the European model of gender and sexuality became central to the making of the modern world order. For instance, as Glenn (2015) shows, when Britain colonized the present-day US, aside from genocide, a prime mechanism of eliminating indigenous people was through assimilating them into bourgeois, British gender norms. Indigenous children were incorporated into gendered schooling systems where boys were trained in farming and trades and girls in domestic skills, boys had to cut their hair and girls had to dress in the colonizers' attire, and the supposed idleness of indigenous men was blamed on indigenous women being so involved in physical labour that they had neglected domestic duties (Glenn 2015). Similar processes occurred elsewhere, for instance in colonial Yoruba society (in present-day Nigeria), where the imposition of Western gender norms meant that those who became gendered as 'women' were denied leadership roles in their communities, as well as control over property and certain economic institutions (see Oyěwùmí 1997).

Together, therefore, intersectionality and decolonial feminism are two approaches that work together, as critical knowledge projects, to destabilize the universalization of white, bourgeois, Western feminism. Importantly, Collins (2019) conceives of these approaches as critical knowledge projects *not* as a means of relegating them to a world of scholasticism, but in order to show the necessary links between epistemology, ontology and social justice. It is through challenging the epistemic principles of white feminism, for instance, that intersectionality is able to expand the horizons of feminist theory to both understand and fight against the gendered racism (and racialized sexism) faced by Black women. Similarly, the coloniality of gender paradigm shows how any feminist epistemology, in order to achieve global equity, has to appreciate how the Western world did not necessarily 'create' gender (Connell 2015; Roberts and Connell 2016), but significantly ruptured how different people thought about and practised gender in a way that incorporated them into the hierarchy of the colonial world order (Lugones 2007). However, as Collins (2019) argues, intersectionality and decolonial feminist theory work together not just in terms of their overall aims, but also in terms of how they methodologically go about achieving their aims of social justice. Namely, both approaches theorize through the use of metaphors, as can be seen through the language of 'intersections' in Crenshaw's (1989) work and 'borderlands' in Anzaldúa's (1987).

Through theorizing in a similar way, Collins (2019) argues that intersectionality and decolonial feminism again *synergize* in the way that they show the possibilities of critical knowledge production. Thus, when Crenshaw (1989) used the term 'intersectionality', it was to highlight how the inequalities faced by Black women in the US cannot be ameliorated by solely race-based or gender-based social policies, but only through social policies which recognize their existence as lying at a particular intersection of racism and sexism. As Crenshaw (1989: 149) famously put it:

> Consider an analogy to traffic in an intersection, coming and going in all four directions. Discrimination, like traffic through an intersection, may flow in one direction, and it may flow in another. If an accident happens in an intersection, it can be caused by cars traveling from any number of directions and, sometimes, from all of them. Similarly, if a Black woman is harmed because she is in the intersection, her injury could result from sex discrimination or race discrimination.

To Crenshaw, therefore, the metaphor of intersections is what enables her to again problematize the generalizability of white women's experiences while critiquing the focus on the Black middle class and Black men in anti-racist legislation. In doing so, the metaphor 'provides a cognitive device for thinking about social inequality within power relations. It asks people to think beyond familiar race-only or gender-only perspectives' (Collins 2019: 29). This metaphor of intersections, moreover, has been useful for feminist thinkers coming from a decolonial standpoint, as we see in the work of Anzaldúa.

Four years prior to Crenshaw's (1989) intervention, Gloria Anzaldúa (2006 [1987]: 317) declared that:

> To survive the Borderlands
> you must live sin fronteras
> be a crossroads.

Writing as a Chicana feminist in the US South, Anzaldúa – just as Crenshaw did several years later – used the metaphor of crossroads, speaking simultaneously to identity and inequality. Connected to this imagery of the crossroads is the metaphor that Anzaldúa is most known for: that of the *borderlands*. Describing her experiences growing up in the Texas–Mexico border area, Anzaldúa invokes the metaphor of the borderlands to highlight the liminal spaces which she acquires in part due to the *non-metaphorical* racism and coloniality of bordering in the United States and beyond. Describing these liminal spaces, Anzaldúa thus comments of herself:

> 'Your allegiance is to La Raza, the Chicano movement', say the members of my race. 'Your allegiance is to the Third World', say my Black and Asian friends. 'Your allegiance is to your gender, to women', say the feminists. Then there's my allegiance to the Gay movement, to the socialist revolution, to the New Age, to magic and the occult. And there's my affinity of literature, to the world of the artist. What am I? A *third world lesbian feminist with Marxist and mystic leanings*. They would chop me up into little fragments and tag each piece with a label. (Quoted in Keating 2009: 2)

These experiences of having people divide parts of her 'into little fragments' and then label these dimensions disparately, and these experiences of having allegiances to different social movements all at the same time, are what encourages Anzaldúa (2006 [1987]: 316) to see the Borderlands as a space where you are simultaneously part of multiple groups while being rejected as an outsider by all of those groups in virtue of being a member of another:

> To live in the Borderlands means you
> are neither hispana india negra española
> ni gabacha, eres mestiza, mulata, half-breed
> caught in the crossfire between camps
> while carrying all five races on your back
> not knowing which side to turn to, run from.

By way of resolution, this is why Anzaldúa (2006 [1987]: 317) declares that 'To survive the Borderlands / you must live sin fronteras, / be a crossroads.' The Borderlands are not just a space of non-existence but a *meeting place* where we attempt to build dialogue and conversations between multiple epistemological traditions *sin fronteras* (without borders). As Collins (2019: 32) thus argues, Anzaldúa's work comes into conversation with the seminal work on US intersectionality in the way that it:

> expands upon the metaphor of intersectionality as a literal crossroads managed by traffic cops to that of the borderlands as a meeting place. [...] Anzaldúa's borderland is simultaneously a way of describing the experiences of navigating marginal, liminal, and outsider within spaces that are created by multiple kinds of borders. This is the potential for 'democratic' exchanges within borderland or intersectional spaces.

Not only do decolonial feminist theory and intersection-ality thus work together to destabilize the universalization of white, Western feminism, and not only do they both theorize through metaphor, but as Collins (2019) shows, they both exist on a similar analytical level as critical knowledge projects. These two critical knowledge projects are not disparate but in epistemic conversation with one another, both capable of learning from each other, and both capable of building on the other's contributions, thus collaboratively moving towards social justice.

A sociology *sin fronteras*?

The discussion in this chapter has been intended to highlight that a conversational, transnational sociology is not just an ideal, but something that has already been realized histori-cally and is still being realized in contemporary sociology. The issue in many cases, therefore, is not that there are no links between thinkers we regularly dismiss as Eurocentric and Southern theory. Rather, the problem is more that the links that do exist are erased by the way that we continue to frame certain thinkers and certain systems of sociological thought, and the way that we reproduce these frames in our sociological writing, research and pedagogy.

It is precisely these ways of 'doing' sociology that the book now turns to in the following chapter, reviewing how the themes outlined in this book can have an influence on the way we practise and teach sociology in the present day. It is here that we may find it useful to return to Anzaldúa's recently invoked concept of living *sin fronteras* – without borders. This is precisely what a conversational sociology would look like. It would be a sociology that – while appreciating the presence of epistemological, ontological and material borders – does not itself seek to (re)produce any of those frontiers. Rather, this decolonial sociology is a sociology that seeks to build connections, and to look for already existing connec-tions that we have collectively erased. How precisely we can work towards this sociology is now our topic of discussion.

Further reading

Articles

Lugones, María. 2007. 'Heterosexualism and the Colonial/ Modern Gender System'. *Hypatia* 22 (1): 186–209.

María Lugones' paper examines how, through colonialism, the West exported and enforced its model of gender and sexuality across the world. Lugones' paper thus challenges the dominant modernity/coloniality paradigm by placing gender at the centre of analysis, showing how the Western model of hetero-patriarchy was integral to the making of the modern world.

Medien, Kathryn. 2019. 'Foucault in Tunisia: The Encounter with Intolerable Power'. *The Sociological Review* 68 (3): 492–507.

Kathryn Medien's paper shows how Foucault's experiences of anti-imperialism in Tunisia radically shaped his theory of power, and his practice of academic activism more generally. In doing so, Medien radically shifts our understanding of Foucault's intellectual trajectory.

Puwar, Nirmal. 2009. 'Sensing a Post-Colonial Bourdieu: An Introduction'. *The Sociological Review* 57 (3): 371–84.

Much like Medien's paper in relation to Foucault, Nirmal Puwar uses this paper to tease out the anti-colonial roots of Bourdieu's social thought. Paying particular attention to Bourdieu's time in Algeria, and his early publications on these experiences and fieldwork, Puwar demonstrates that anti-colonialism helped shape much of Bourdieu's intellectual apparatus.

Books

Du Bois, W. E. Burghardt. 2014 [1935]. *Black Reconstruction in America: An Essay Toward a History of the Part which Black Folk Played in the Attempt to Reconstruct Democracy in America, 1860–1880*. Oxford: Oxford University Press.

W. E. B. Du Bois' book offers a critique of racial capitalism that brings insights from classical Marxism together with the realities of both racism in the United States and the colonial world order more generally. It is an example of how a thinker has expanded the scope of a classical, bifurcated tradition of social thought to critically account for the realities of coloniality.

Shari'ati, Ali., 1980. *Marxism and Other Western Fallacies: An Islamic Critique*. Markfield: Islamic Foundation Press.

Ali Shari'ati's book launches a critique of Western social thought and humanism, focusing particularly on existentialism and Marxism. Both traditions, he argues, ignore the spiritual, material and revolutionary dynamics of religion. By contrast, Shari'ati does not merely dismiss Western Marxism and existentialism, but incorporates them into his religious sociology built around the principles of Shi'a Islam.

Conclusion: Sociology and the Decolonial Option

When Raewyn Connell (1997) published 'Why Is Classical Theory Classical?' in the *American Journal of Sociology*, Randall Collins (1997) replied that the attempt to ground the emergence of sociology in the world of colonialism was nothing more than a 'sociological guilt trip'. However, as I hope has been visible throughout this book, the aim of decolonizing sociology is not to generate a sense of individual or collective guilt, but to achieve a degree of epistemic justice and make sociology a more critical discipline.

One way that decolonial sociology attempts to deepen the criticality of the discipline is simply by turning sociology's tools on itself. We have seen this in feminist standpoint theory, where scholars have highlighted the masculinity of canons and viewpoints in the discipline (Harding 1987);[1] we have seen this in the sociology of race, through the highlighting of the whiteness of the dominant sociological canon and viewpoints (Du Bois 1898);[2] and we have seen this in Black feminist thought, in terms of the relegation of Black feminist thinkers as 'outsiders within' sociology (Collins 1998).[3] All of these approaches have essentially highlighted sociology's basic premise that all knowledge – including sociological knowledge – is socially situated. Decolonizing sociology, in this regard, is simply another approach that shows how sociology is a situated form of knowledge production. The difference is that it looks at how sociology emerged in the world of empires, colonialism and imperialism, and continues to be positioned in the relationships of coloniality.

The basic premise of this book, therefore, has been that through embracing the 'decolonial option', sociology can become a more critical discipline. In using the term 'decolonial option', I am borrowing directly from Mignolo and Walsh (2018: 224), when they argue that:

It has been suggested that decoloniality should be understood as an imperative rather than an option, for option may imply voluntarism. My argument is that [...] there is nothing but options, options within the imaginary of modernity and options within decolonial imaginaries. Accordingly you choose an option in full awareness of the chart or you are chosen by one of the existing options that you take, willingly or not, as the truth, the correct or right one.

We in sociology need to choose the decolonial option, to accept it as 'the truth, the correct or right [option]', if we are to collectively sustain a practice of epistemic justice and deepen the analytic capabilities of our discipline. The requirement to embrace the decolonial option in sociology becomes especially apparent when we consider one of the central problems of our time – the climate crisis.

Embracing the decolonial option: sociology, coloniality and the climate crisis

I am writing this section of the book in early 2020. Already this year, Puerto Rico has suffered its most deadly earthquake in the past one hundred years. In the past year (2019), Cyclone Idai – the most powerful cyclone recorded in the southern hemisphere – swept through Southeast Africa, creating humanitarian crises in Mozambique, Zimbabwe and Malawi, while lack of rainfall created mass water shortages in India, and a record high heatwave in Southern Australia led to the burning of vast amounts of land, including much of the Tasmanian forest. While it is true that sociology is not simply a vehicle for forming social policy, sociology does need some form of engagement with the world if it is to avoid being relegated to the realm of abstract philosophy.[4] The state of the earth's climate means that, regardless of one's views of the scope of sociology, it is a realistic possibility that very soon there may be no world within which we can do sociology to begin with; thus the centrality of the climate crisis to sociology.

Despite the centrality of the climate crisis to our collective lives on earth, it is a relatively understudied area in Western sociology.[5] Looking through the *American Sociology Review*, for instance, no journal articles have been published with 'climate change' or 'climate crisis' in their titles; the *Annual Review of Sociology* has one paper published in 2020 (Dietz et al. 2020); while *The American Journal of Sociology* returns five papers, although all of these are reviews of manuscripts rather than being pieces of discrete research. Between three of the most renowned sociology journals, this means there is only *one paper* producing discrete research that has 'climate change/crisis' in the title, and it is a review paper that seeks to pave a way forward in the discipline rather than producing empirical research itself (Dietz et al. 2020).

Despite its relative neglect in the Western standpoint, climate change and climate crises have been central in the Southern standpoint – this is one of the first reasons in why embracing a decolonial option is necessary to sociologize about the climate crisis. Thus, when Alatas (2006: 20) sketched out why we need an autonomous sociology that breaks from the Western tradition, one of his points was that this would allow us to reflect on issues such as the climate crisis – or particularly 'degradation of the environment' – that are central to the lives of people in the Global South. Similarly, in calling for a de-linking from Northern theory, Connell (2018: 403) points out that in the Global South it is 'hard to get worked up about reflexive modernity or shifting subjectivities' when you are facing daily realities of phenomena such as the 'climate disaster'.

Part of the reason why climate crises have been focused on within the Southern standpoint is because decolonial thinkers spotted the link between modernity/coloniality and the destruction of the environment in the name of capital accumulation. Almost a century ago, Du Bois (1954: 3) commented on how the driving logic of neo-colonial capitalism was 'private profit from low wages of colored workers and low prices for *priceless raw materials* over the earth' (emphasis added). As Du Bois picks out, modernity/ coloniality – fostered through the actions of empires which wanted to hoard, capitalize and profit from the world's resources – was always committed to the destruction of the environment in the name of economic growth.[6] Dussel summarizes this logic of modernity/coloniality and environmental destruction when he comments that:

> Capitalism, mediation of exploitation and accumulation (effect of the world-system), is later on transformed into an independent system that from out of its own self-referential and autopoietic logic can destroy Europe and its periphery, *even the entire planet.* (Dussel 1999: 17, emphasis added)

As pinpointed from decolonial thinkers, from Du Bois to Dussel, we are in a situation where something that was set in motion through European colonialism – a desire for capital accumulation at the expense of planetary destruction – continues to have a disproportionate impact on the Global South.[7] Furthermore, given the cultural repertoire of individualism that sweeps across the Western world, many Western responses to the climate crisis revolve around individual consumption habits that end up reinscribing relations of coloniality: such as switching to electric cars, which largely relies on child labour in places such as the Democratic Republic of Congo,[8] or switching to a plant-based diet, which often relies on near-free labour in the South such as we see with Indian women picking cashews for less than 30p a day to meet the rising Western demand for non-dairy alternatives.[9] This is why thinkers such as Wynter (2003) see the climate crisis as a key example of the dominance of 'man' (defined as supra-humans – those seen to belong in the white, Western world) and 'human' (the various 'species' of sub-people created through colonialism, whether that be Black, brown or indigenous people and so on). Both in the realities of the climate crisis, and in Western responses to it, those in the Global South – those who, according to Wynter, count as 'human' rather than man – are the people suffering the most.[10] As Wynter (2003: 260–1) clarifies:

> all our present [...] struggles over the environment, global warming, severe climate change, the sharply unequal distribution of the earth resources (20 percent of the world's peoples own 80 percent of its resources, consume two-thirds of its food, and are responsible for 75 percent of its ongoing pollution, with this leading to two billion of earth's peoples living relatively affluent lives while four billion still live on the edge of hunger and immiseration, to the dynamic of overconsumption on the part of the rich techno-industrial North paralleled by that of overpopulation on the part of the dispossessed poor, still partly agrarian worlds of the South) – these are all differing facets of the central ethnoclass Man vs. Human struggle.

Given such recognition of the link between modernity/ coloniality and environmental destruction, notions of a climate crisis are not something new to the Southern standpoint, but have been within this standpoint since various people have been subjugated through colonialism. This is why some social scientists have called for us to collectively learn from, for instance, indigenous people who have been dealing with climate crises from day one of the birth of colonial power.[11] Such social scientists argue that indigenous people across the world have had to deal with the destruction of their environments by settler colonialists, in the name of capital accumulation,[12] and therefore that they are the best-placed people from whom to learn about how to deal with climate crises. As Franco Cassano (2010: 214) puts it 'a world suffocated by unlimited growth needs to discover the wisdom of a way of life that does not seek to violate the earth but rather recognizes the limits of exploitation'. Indeed, other social scientists have built upon this idea of the West learning from others as a key way that we can build a new form of planetary universal humanism, and that, by recognizing our shared existence as finite beings, humanity can form a new horizontal collectivity. As Namita Goswami states (2013: 106):

> climate change, as the singular crisis putting at risk the very possibility of human culture, as we have known it, is the ground upon which a new understanding of global multicultural reality and postcolonial antiracist theory must be developed. I argue that this global multi-cultural reality must include the cultural reality of our lives as animals.

For the sake of this book's scope, I am not going to explicitly focus on what we – collectively across the planet – can learn from various different people about how to tackle climate crisis. However, from a sociological viewpoint and the viewpoint in this book, it is worth noting that the tradition of Western sociology not only largely ignores the climate crisis in its overall standpoint, but also lacks the sociological tools to be able to think critically about the issue in the first place. This blind spot comes not just from the failure to recognize modernity/coloniality and its links to environmental destruction, but also in terms of the commitment to substantivism and a limited humanism in Western sociology, which creates a clear binary between 'people' and 'nature'. As Chakrabarty (2009b: 207) has commented, the Western tradition has been predicated on a clear division between 'human and natural histories', in which humans are said to have an *interactive* relationship with the natural world. By contrast, the climate catastrophe requires us to think about how humans are themselves 'a force of nature in the geological sense' (Chakrabarty 2009b:

207). In order to properly theorize this relationship between humanity and nature, we need to go beyond Western social thought's commitment to substantivism.

Through a substantivism – a focus on *things* – Western sociology fails to grasp the relations that link humans with the wider environment. As Mignolo and Walsh (2018: 148) argue, this focus on 'things' is something quite unique to Western thought:

> Most of culture and civilizations on the planet *see relations while in the West we are taught to see entities, things. Relations* could not be called ontological. If the vocabulary wants to be preserved then one needs to talk about *relationalogy* (discourses on/about relationality of the living universe).

Through this substantivist approach, Western sociology has significant problems with situating humans in their wider relations with the environment. Humans may be social animals, but we are only capable of being social animals in virtue of some kind of environment. Even critical traditions within Western sociology – such as Marxism, and the critical theory of Horkheimer and Adorno (2002 [1944]) – may have paid attention to humankind's desire to control nature, but still instil a binary between humanity and nature to begin with. If we are to generate a critical sociological approach towards understanding and responding to the climate crisis, we thus need different understandings of humanity, nature and agency that transcend the limitations of bifurcated Western thought. As Achille Mbembe (2016: 42) thus exclaims, we need to 'rethink the human not from the perspective of its mastery of the Creation as we used to, but from the perspective of its finitude and its possible extinction'. Decolonial thinkers from different locations have been doing this very theorizing on humanism, nature and agency.

You may recall that in the previous chapter, for instance, we encountered the work of Ali Shari'ati. Importantly, Shari'ati's approach to humanism and nature was formed through his Shi'a Islamic sociology. Thus, in Shari'ati's (1980) sociological system, there is no binary between humankind and nature, because people are simultaneously nature and subjectivity in one body, as captured through the principle of *Tauhid*. As Shari'ati thus claims:

> Islam, however, not only resolves the oppositions of nature, man, and God through the principle of Tauhid, but also, by proclaiming the truth that human subjectivity and material nature are both *different signs or manifestations of a single sublime essence, transcends the oppositions of idea and matter, and of man and nature*. Even while considering the essential human reality and material actuality as two distinct principle, *it establishes a fundamental bond, an existential relation, between them, in regarding the two as arising from a single origin.* (Shari'ati 1980: 43, emphasis added)

As we can see in Shari'ati's paradigm, there is an 'existential relation' between 'man and nature'. Rather than seeing a bifurcation between the two phenomena – as does the Western humanism Shari'ati is criticizing in this paragraph (and in which he groups French existentialism, Western Marxism and Soviet communism) – Shari'ati shows that humans are themselves partly physical, material, 'natural' beings. To see a bifurcation between humanity and nature would thus be to deny humanity one of its essences.

The idea of 'nature' being an essence of humanity is also espoused in indigenous epistemologies. For instance, Manulani Aluli Meyer (2008) highlights the Hawaiian epistemology, and the way that land and environment become cornerstones of what it means to be human. As Meyer shows, this is even captured in how the Hawaiian greeting of *aloha* – translating literally as 'to share breath' – is part of a way of life which constantly situates humans as being parts within a larger, natural environment. Meyer (2008: 219) clarifies:

> Indigenous people are all about place. Land/*aina*, defined as 'that which feeds,' is the everything to our sense of

love, joy, and nourishment. Land is our mother. *This is not a metaphor.* For the Native Hawaiians speaking of knowledge, land was the central theme that drew forth all others. You came from a place. You grew in a place and you had a relationship with that place. *This is an epistemological idea.* Because of the high mobility of Americans and billboards as childhood scenery, many find this idea difficult to comprehend. Land/ocean shapes my thinking, my way of being, and my priorities of what is of value.

As Meyer highlights, through the Hawaiian perspective, 'land' is construed not only as a necessary feature for human existence, thought and knowledge, but also as something *within which* humans are situated and thus are part of. Land, therefore, in this thought is not just a physical thing but becomes part of wider epistemological-ontological principles; that is, just as 'humans' become situated in nature, 'nature' is also articulated through humans – thus the falsity of the binary.[13] As Meyer (2008: 219) states:

Land is more than a physical place. It is an idea that engages knowledge and contextualizes knowing. It is the key that turns the doors inward to reflect on how space shapes us. Space as fullness, as interaction, as thoughts planted. It is not about emptiness but about *consciousness.* It is an epistemological idea because it conceptualizes those things of value to embed them in a *context.* Land is more than just a physical locale; it is a mental one that becomes water on the rock of our being.

The reason why Shari'ati's and Meyer's cases are pertinent to this discussion is because they both show the need for a shift in sociology's dominant epistemological-ontological frameworks. Tackling issues such as the climate crisis in sociology involves battling not only the coloniality of power – in terms of the climate inequalities between the Global

North and South – but also the *coloniality of knowledge*. Western sociology is limited by a specific form of humanism that commits itself to individualism and anthropocentrism, creating a rigid binary between humans and nature. It is this bifurcated logic which allows humans to treat nature as an external world that can be manipulated, controlled and ultimately subjected in the name of capital development (itself a means for the supposed 'development' of humanity). Without embracing the decolonial option – which recognizes the links between modernity/coloniality and environmental destruction, as well as offering concepts of nature and humanism that move beyond a clear binary – sociology loses the ability to talk about and frame a central problem of our time, the climate crisis, in critical ways.

Widening the scope of sociological methodologies

Despite Shari'ati and Meyer widening our understandings of nature and humanism – through Islamic and Hawaiian social thought respectively – and deepening our sociological capabilities in doing so, these kinds of thinkers, ideas and general *approaches to doing sociology* do not tend to make it onto sociology syllabi across the world. Shari'ati's (1980, 1986) regular citing of the Quran and of the teachings of the Prophet and First Imam, for instance, is not deemed by Western eyes to be an acceptable sociological methodology. This is precisely the reason why Foucault (2010 [1978]: 209), who saw great value in the spiritual sociology being developed by Shari'ati, also knew that it would not be received in Western social thought, saying: 'I can already hear the French laughing, but I know that they are wrong.'

What this shows is that decolonizing sociology, or sustaining a decolonial sociology, necessitates that we widen our scope of sociological methodologies. Following Maggie Walter and Chris Andersen (2013), 'methodology' here refers not to particular methods (e.g. interviews, statistics, ethnography etc), nor to 'types' of method (e.g. quantitative or qualitative), but to the overall approach taken towards sociological research. In sociology, 'methodologies' therefore refer to the valuation of certain questions over others, the frame within which 'data are collected, analysed, and interpreted [...] how, when, and where the data are gathered; how they are explored; and how the resulting data are interpreted and, significantly, eventually used' (Walter and Andersen 2013: 10).

One way that decolonizing sociology encourages us to widen the scope of sociological methodologies is simply through acknowledging that sociological research is always situated. There is a strong tradition – especially stemming from the Weberian (1981) and Durkheimian (2010 [1953], 2014 [1938]) schools of thought – that sociology ought to be conducted from a value-neutral position. Through the work of standpoint theorists we have already mentioned, as well as through larger 'turns' such as with poststructuralism and postmodernism, qualitative sociology has been fairly receptive to the idea that sociological methodologies are situated and value-laden.[14] On the other hand, quantitative sociology has remained more hesitant to collectively embrace the idea that even 'sociology with numbers' is a situated practice with specific value commitments.[15]

By contrast, in *Indigenous Statistics*, Walter and Andersen (2013) show how quantitative sociology too is part of various situated methodologies. Writing from indigenous standpoints, the authors begin from the point that statistical methods – a common tool in quantitative sociology – have a pernicious history with indigenous people across the world, echoing Linda Tuhiwai Smith's (2008 [1999]: 1) point that:

> The word itself, 'research', is probably one of the dirtiest words in the indigenous world's vocabulary. When mentioned in many indigenous contexts, it stirs up silence, it conjures up bad memories, it raises a smile that is knowing and distrustful. It is so powerful that indigenous people even write poetry about research. The ways in which scientific research is implicated in the worst excesses of colonialism remains a powerful remembered history for many of the world's colonized

peoples. It is a history that still offends the deepest sense
of our humanity.

Thus, across the world, statistics have been a key mechanism
for enforcing state definitions and control of indigenous
people.[16] In many Latin American countries throughout the
twentieth century, for instance, states have tried to define
indigeneity in a way that minimizes the census count of
indigenous people (for instance, by equating indigeneity
with living in particular places, or being fluent in only an
indigenous language) as a means for reproducing myths that
the nation is racially mixed, and not divided along racialized
contours (see Loveman 2014). Through this practice, we can
see that quantitative methods can be incorporated into sociological methodologies that are far from value-neutral, but are
instead connected to wider racial projects.

Coming from a different angle, Walter and Andersen
(2013) thus also propose a practice of 'indigenous statistics'
– a methodology that makes use of quantitative sociology for
the purpose of empowering indigenous people. This methodology starts from the premise that we can put an indigenous
standpoint at the heart of the methodological approach, and
that 'value-neutral' sociology – while being impossible – is
also a sociology that itself has no value. Through such 'indigenous statistics', the sociological methodology thus becomes
part of a wider anti-colonial/decolonial project of speaking
back against the erasure of indigenous histories and the
devaluation of indigenous people and knowledges that takes
place through settler colonialisms.[17] Walter and Andersen
argue that this use of statistics to work against the epistemic
logic of settler colonialism can take place through the indigenous practice of *nayri kati* (good numbers). This practice of
nayri kati, Walter and Andersen argue, changes the way that
we ask questions about indigeneity and indigenous life. Thus,
while Western methodologies may use statistics to investigate
questions pertaining to 'indigenous enrolment at Australian
universities', an indigenous statistics approach would instead
use statistics to look at 'How well do Australian universities
incorporate indigenous participation?' or 'How effective are

the government's programmes to incorporate indigenous student and staff participation and cultural presence in their universities?' (Walter and Andersen 2013). Similarly, while Western methodologies may value questions pertaining to indigenous self-segregation, an indigenous statistics approach would ask questions surrounding issues of how settlers and non-indigenous people construe and socialize with indigenous people (Walter and Andersen 2013).

Central to this notion of indigenous statistics, therefore, is the idea of reflexively putting particular standpoints at the heart of the methodology. An extension of this point is that given that different groups have different standpoints, different groups may have different sociological methodologies – that is, different approaches to *how to do sociology*. When working towards a decolonial sociology, we therefore need to be thinking about these different methodologies across the world, and how many of these methodologies enable us to produce different, new and more critical types of knowledge from what is produced within the confines of Western social thought. To use the previous example of the climate crisis, for instance, an indigenous statistics approach would be able to shift our attention to overlooked phenomena by placing the indigenous standpoint at the heart of our research process. Such research could, for instance, highlight links between capital accumulation, climate change and the indigenous who suffer from this destruction of the climate, by questioning the relationship between a nation like Brazil's or Canada's[18] GDP growth and the levels of air pollution in indigenous reservations. Through this practice of indigenous statistics, therefore, an established method can be adopted for anti-colonial means.

Beyond indigenous statistics, we also have the wider (although more qualitatively focused) notion of indigenous methodologies.[19] Again, these methodologies centre indigenous standpoints, where indigenous worldviews are not something just to be studied 'in itself', but also an epistemology which guides the overall research and valuation process. As Linda Tuhiwai Smith (2008 [1999]) points out in *Decolonizing Methodologies*, settlers may 'research' indigenous life through pseudo-ethnography or statistical observation, but indigenous research takes an alternative approach. Namely, indigenous methodologies recognize the variety of ways that knowledge is produced and social life sustained, ways that escape the attention of dominant sociological methods and approaches valued in the West. For instance, Smith points out that storytelling and the oral tradition are key ways of doing indigenous research. As Smith (2008 [1999]: 144–5) clarifies, such a practice of story-telling is a central way that the history of indigenous people and indigenous life is able to be transmitted across genera-tions, thus allowing such knowledge to avoid the Western epistemicide:

> Each individual story is powerful. But the point about the stories is not that they simply tell a story, or tell a story simply. […] For many indigenous writers stories are ways of passing down the beliefs and values of a culture in the hope that the new generations will treasure them and pass the story down further. The story and the story teller both serve to connect the past with the future, one generation with the other, the land with the people and the people with the story.

Smith's comment on incorporating storytelling into indigenous methodologies connects with other sociologists working in different traditions. For instance, we have already mentioned Akiwowo (1986, 1999) in this book, and his attempts to ground an indigenous sociology that explores themes such as self, community and agency through the Yoruba oral tradition. Speaking from what they see as an African context, other scholars such as Olutayo (2014) have therefore argued that we need to incorporate proverbs into our sociological methodologies. Such proverbs may not be ascribed importance in Western social thought, but across different cultures in the Global South they are used as forms of local knowledge of social processes. As Olutayo (2014: 235) thus argues:

Proverbs present deep meanings that contextualize and structure embedded social relations, social structure, culture, and accompanying development within the contextualized meaning of the immediate local/culture group.

Building upon this approach, Olutayo thus highlights various ways that proverbs can be incorporated into sociological research in a non-Orientalist fashion. One such example is in the principle of group solidarity and collectivity among different cultures, and their rejection of Western bourgeois individualism. Thus, Olutayo (2014: 235) cites the Yoruban proverb that 'A tree does not make a forest' and the Akan proverb that 'A person is not a palm-tree that he should be self-complete [or self-sufficient].' Olutayo (2014: 235) argues that these proverbs are representative of the wider saying 'common among Africans' that 'One hand cannot lift a load up to the head. The left hand washes the right hand and the right hand washes the left for the hands to be clean. It is when all hands come together that confidence (independence) exudes.' From these proverbs, Olutayo provides insights into social processes concerning sharing common interests, forming interpersonal bonds and rejecting individualism. Despite the fact that these proverbs can tell us a lot about social processes, and how these social processes are mediated through local knowledge – which are the remits of sociology and microsociology respectively (Collins 1981) – these forms of local knowledge are excluded from dominant sociological methodologies.

Time to fire the canon?

With such critical knowledges – from indigenous statistics and stories through to African proverbs – falling through the gaps of Western sociology, we have to ask ourselves why the Western approach deserves its declared universality. Through thinking about different sociological conceptions of humanism and nature, and then different sociological methodologies, one thing becomes clear: there are multiple sociological systems, and multiple ways to do sociology. As with any system of hierarchization, the valuation of these different systems and ways of doing sociology is *not natural* but grounded in social processes – in this case, the processes of the coloniality of power and knowledge. If we agree that sociology's hierarchy and valuation of various knowledges and methodologies are themselves grounded in the wider matrix of colonial relations, we thus need to ask ourselves: 'Does sociology need a canon?' and, perhaps an even more difficult question: 'Can sociology have a canon while claiming to be decolonial?'

In 2007, Connell published the formative book *Southern Theory*. This book simultaneously showed the imperial roots of sociology and highlighted the plethora of sociological work and sociologists working from the context of the Global South (Connell 2007a). Several years later, in 2013, *Political Power and Social Theory* led a special issue on Connell's book, entitled 'Decentering Social Theory'. One of the criticisms of Connell's book in this special issue came from Reed (2013), who argued that while Connell's work is admirable, it went about challenging sociology's metrocentrism in the wrong way. Namely, Reed argues that *Southern Theory* ended up challenging the Northern or Western canon through building a new canon altogether – a canon composed of different sociological traditions and sociologists in a Global South context. In Reed's understanding, *Southern Theory* almost seems to be presenting an arbitrary canon – where the canonical sociologists are only connected in virtue of being from or working within the Global South – in order to displace the other arbitrary, Western canon.

This critique of *Southern Theory* is not one that I agree with, as I read the book as an attempt to decentre Northern theory, to challenge its universality, and simply to show us how much sociological knowledge and how many methodologies are erased or obfuscated by the Eurocentric standpoint. However, Reed's (2013) critique does feed into an issue that is recurring in discussions and practices of moving towards a decolonial sociology. In particular, those of us working towards a decolonial sociology have to consider what problems arise once we start to construct a decolonial canon in sociology, and whether forming such a canon is either consistent with, or desirable from, a decolonial approach. Puwar (2019), for instance, has highlighted how the recent 'decolonial wave' in sociology has resulted in a set of authors being canonized, most of whom work in the Global North. Such authors, Puwar argues, become a sort of global ambassador for Southern or decolonial theory, as they 'bring' Southern theory into Northern institutions. While Puwar sees no issues in the work of such authors, and neither is she critiquing the ethics and intentions of their work, she points out that this new decolonial canon and practice in sociology seem to reproduce the hegemony of the Global North over the South, as it is the 'translators' of the Southern theory who become the highly esteemed academics, rather than the Southern theorist themselves. 'Those who set themselves up in this role', Bhambra (2020: 459) clarifies, 'whether wittingly or not, can become complicit in the reproduction of particular hierarchies – hierarchies that they otherwise contest.'

Of course, some within sociology and social science are quite up front about wanting to produce a 'new' canon in their project of decoloniality. Mignolo (2007, 2011b), for instance, argues that you can shape an entire decolonial canon from its trajectory from two thinkers: Waman Puma and Quobna Ottobah. As they were anti-colonial thinkers against the Spanish empire in the sixteenth century and the British empire in the eighteenth century respectively, Mignolo (2011b: 53) argues that Puma's and Ottobah's commitments to relationality, critiquing modernity/coloniality and centring the agency of the colonized make them the foundation stone for later decolonial scholars, institutions and movements, including:

W. E. B. Dubois, José Carlos Mariátegui, Amílcar Cabral, Aimé Césaire, Frantz Fanon, Fausto Reinaga, Vine Deloria Jr., Rigoberta Menchú, Gloria Anzaldúa, the

Brazilian *Sem Terras* movement (Landless Movement), the Zapatistas in Chiapas, the Indigenous and Afro movements in Bolivia, Ecuador, and Colombia, the World Social Forum and the Social Forum of the Americas.

In sociology more specifically, scholars calling for indigenous or autonomous sociologies base their whole approach on needing a 'new' canon – as we see with Alatas (2010, 2014) calling for an Asian tradition of sociology based on a canon of Rizal and Khaldūn, or Adésínà (2006) calling for a South African tradition of sociology formed around a canon of Steve Biko, Goven Mbeki, Bernard Magubane, Archie Mafeje and Fatima Meer. In *Sociological Theory Beyond the Canon*, Alatas and Sinha (2017) even go as far as to admit that their aim is 'to introduce non western thinkers to the canon in an aim to universalise the canon' – and thus add thinkers such as Khaldūn, Benoy Kumar Sarkar, Said Nursi and Pandita Ramabai Saraswati alongside the more known figures such as Marx, Weber and Durkheim.

These efforts at building a decolonial canon – broadly and within sociology – show a basic fact within academic fields: that canons help us to form a 'disciplinary home'.[20] It is through having a canon that an academic field can show what concepts, questions, methods and theories we value and position ourselves with/against.[21] Indeed, this is precisely one of the reasons why 'the canon' becomes such a key focus for decolonial critique across and within many disciplines, including sociology. Through critiquing, or displacing, a disciplinary canon, we are able to reshape the whole field. In the case of sociology, reshaping this whole field would allow us to incorporate in it people and systems of thought that would not primarily be allowed access under previous conditions. It is precisely this reshaping of the structure, and therefore of the scope of 'acceptable' sociology, that would allow new epistemologies and methodologies to flourish within sociology – such as Shari'ati's religious sociology, doing sociology through proverbs or incorporating stories from indigenous oral traditions.

A problem then arises when we consider what to do after decentring the dominant canon, and beginning to restructure the field. After displacing a canon in our mission of decoloniality, can we instigate a new one without reproducing layers of epistemic inequality? If canons are connected to processes of knowledge valuation and hierarchization, and decoloniality is about fostering horizontal conversations across different epistemic traditions, then is the idea of a decolonial canon in sociology contradictory? When engaging with these questions, I think there are two interconnected problems worth thinking about.

Firstly, there is the issue of individualism. If we build a new decolonial canon in sociology, do we end up reproducing the focus on individual thinkers rather than flows and systems of decolonial thought and practices? Part of the problem currently in sociology's canon is that we are presented with sets of thinkers, largely divorced from their lived worlds. This is what makes it easy for sociology textbooks and curricula to, for instance, teach Marxism as the sociology of Marx, rather than seeing its connections with anti-colonial thinkers such as Du Bois. It is also this focus on individual theorists that makes it easy to sever the links between canonical thinkers and their decolonial roots – as we saw in the previous chapter with Bourdieu and Foucault. We thus need to deal with the issue of how to instigate any kind of decolonial canon without giving too much primacy to individual theorists, divorced from their connections with lived realities and exchanges with other thinkers.

This connects with the point of what Collins (2019: 123) identifies as 'coining narratives'. Part of the colonial logic we have seen historically is that discovery of a territory implies naming rights over it. Of course, these 'naming rights' – given to Western empires – paid no attention to the reality that people were already living in these 'discovered' places, and already had names for themselves and their spaces. Collins points out that as soon as we start equating individual theorists with particular theoretical paradigms, we end up reproducing this logic of discovery and naming rights, thus doing a disservice to the thinkers who have already lived on these epistemic grounds despite not necessarily using the same language. While Collins uses the example of intersectionality, I think we can broaden out the point to think about decolonial sociology more broadly. Thus, Collins (2019: 122), speaking about how it is regularly said that Crenshaw 'coined' the term intersectionality, argues that:

> This origin story inserts intersectionality into a familiar colonial narrative that positions Crenshaw as the intrepid explorer who, because she discovers virgin territory, gets naming rights. Yet from the perspective of the colonized, such colonial narratives also signal power relations of domination that begin with discovery, move on to conquest, and end with ongoing pacification. Identifying intersectionality's narrative with its moment of academic discovery assigns value to when its explorers brought home something of interest to colonists. Given this context, who gets to tell intersectionality's story? And what story will they tell?

Opening this up to the topic of decoloniality and sociology more broadly, Collins thus encourages us to think about who gets left out, and who gets to tell particular stories, once we start equating individual thinkers with particular concepts. Again, this constitutes a significant problem for any canon formation in a decolonial sociology. After all, we cannot teach and discuss a concept (for instance, modernity/coloniality) without teaching or discussing theorists who have used the term (e.g. Quijano), and neither can you teach a concept by listing every and any theorist whose work bears any epistemic relation to it. Even if we do create a decolonial canon which gives primacy to systems of ideas (e.g. the coloniality of gender, modernity/coloniality etc.), we thus need to be cognizant that our vision of the people we see as being pioneers of such theories can end up reproducing layers of epistemic injustice or inequality. This critique feeds into the wider point that no decolonial scholar ought to be put 'beyond' criticism, and that a critical scepticism is healthy for the discipline of sociology. While putting Du Bois and Fanon at the centre of sociology curricula on modernity, for instance, may be an important practice, neither of these thinkers can be seen as being *the* answer to all of sociology's problems. Du Bois, for instance, has been accused of elitism in his thesis that a 'talented tenth' should emerge to lead Black folks in the United States (see Sall and Khan 2017), while Fanon has been criticized for neglecting the violence towards Black women in colonialism (Lane and Mahdi 2013). While building a decolonial canon may appear to be a justifiable course of action, therefore, we may continue to reproduce inequalities if we merely put new scholars on the sociological pedestal.

Rather than attempting to systematically answer these problems with regard to decoloniality and canons in sociology, I would leave them as open thinking points. Decoloniality is not something that can ever be fully achieved, but is an ongoing process.[22] In sociology, one of these ongoing processes of decoloniality is navigating between, on the one hand, trying to change the structure and valuation system of the discipline, and, on the other hand, wanting to avoid reinscribing any logic of coloniality or inequality more broadly in creating a new canon when sustaining this structural transformation of sociology. In this spirit of thinking of decoloniality as an *ongoing process* rather than something that can be concretely 'achieved', I want to conclude this book by listing seven points for what we can collectively do, and constantly be asking ourselves and thinking about, to sustain a decolonial movement within sociology. This is by no means a blueprint for decolonizing sociology, but rather an invitation for ongoing, reflexive practice and questioning – a reflexivity that is already being practised by many across the globe[23] – that can help us to build a collective, horizontal sociology.

1. Situate the development of sociology in the field of colonial-imperial relations

This book's introductory chapter highlighted how sociology was formally institutionalized in the nineteenth and early twentieth centuries, when the discipline became deeply entangled in the wider practices and logics of empires, colonialism and imperialism. Sociology was thus integral in producing and reproducing the whole mechanism of knowledge production that can be labelled as the *colonial episteme*. This involved sociologists reproducing the myth of colonial difference, through arguing that those in the colonies were 'backwards' in terms of civilization and development (as was done by, for example, Durkheim, Weber, Keller, W. I. Thomas and Elias), and through arguing that colonialism could uplift colonized people into a higher form of economic and social life (as was done by, for instance, Marx, Park and Giddings).

Importantly, this history of sociology is *not* just a history. Rather, the fact that sociology developed at the high point of colonialism, and produced, internalized and reproduced the colonial episteme, is integral to the logic of the discipline today. Through colonialism, the 'West' was able to position itself as the epistemic centre of the world. This is the very same logic that allows sociologists now to collectively reproduce a canon of theorists (including Marx, Weber and Durkheim – each of whom reproduced the myth of colonial difference and civilizational backwardness) as if sociology only happens in the West. The especial valuation of the West is what allows for sociologists – including those in the South – to still assume that all our theory and key contributions are generated in the Global North, while the South merely exists as a pool for data.[24] This centrality of the West is what allows sociologists to still split the study of the West and Western modernity from its imperial, colonial relations – such as with Mann's (2012a, 2012b, 2012c, 2012d) *The Sources of Social Power*, which aims to provide us with a history of power in human societies, but provides analyses largely of Great Britain, Europe and the United States, without integrating analysis of how all of these nation states were in fact global empires.[25]

Without appreciating the past of the discipline, and the continuity of colonial relations of power under the process of coloniality, we fail to fully understand how our discipline

works now. Of course, the reason why much of this bifurcation is so common is because of the assumption that we
can universalize from the West to the rest of the world.[26]
Analysing 'the rest' of the world, let alone the links between
the West and the rest, is not necessary for generating universal
social theory.[27]

2. De-universalize any canon

Instigating a decolonial sociology, therefore, necessitates a
provincializing or de-universalizing of sociology. This does
not mean that the authors we typically associate with the
sociology canon have to be banned from textbooks and
curricula. Instead, it implies a greater degree of analysing the
context of the authors' works, and the extent to which their
supposedly universal theories actually speak to a very specific
socio-historical context in which we can situate their social
thought. As Alatas and Sinha (2001) remark on teaching
classical social theory in Singapore, through rejecting the idea
that the Eurocentric canon is *universal*, we are not implying
that authors within this canon are not *useful* for sociology.

Take, for instance, the holy trinity of Marx, Weber and
Durkheim. Each of these three thinkers is often presented to
us as offering some kind of universal theory of modernity or
capitalism.[28] However, each of these three thinkers largely
analysed such social processes in the context of Western
societies, and failed to engage critically with either alternative
modernities in the South, or the links between modernity
in the West and the underdevelopment of the rest of the
world through colonialism.[29] Thus, each of Marx, Weber
and Durkheim – rather than producing universal theories
– actually relied on the myth of colonial difference in order
to buttress his understanding of *European* modernity and
capitalism. For instance, Marx (1973 [1939]) argued that
'Asiatic' societies lacked the social and economic organization
to transition into capitalism; Weber (1959, 2000 [1958])
contrasted the Protestant ethic (a prerequisite for capitalism)
with the idleness or spiritualism of Hinduism, Islam and
Confucianism; while Durkheim (2008 [1912]) studied

Aboriginal people as a means of contrasting pre-modern and modern societies. Each of these three thinkers generalized the colonized world as being *pre-modern* in order to present his analysis of modernity and capitalism in the West as being universally true. Situating canonical authors in their context thus allows us to assess what is *useful* in their paradigms of thought, rather than assuming the universality of their works.

In provincializing the canon, the task for decolonial sociology thus becomes to not just focus on individual thinkers but put them into conversation with wider circulations of ideas. Again, this does not necessitate burning the books of previously canonized authors. Instead of teaching a class on 'the sociology of Marx', for instance, you could teach a class on social class and the industrial revolution. This does not require a bifurcated account of capitalism as something that happened in the West because of the internal structure of the West, but, for instance, could be a course that also incorporates the work of Du Bois (2014 [1935]) or Williams (1944), and the importance of enslavement and colonialism to industrial development and class formation across Europe. Similarly, a course on Weber could be recast as a course on religious ethics and the development of capitalism, which would easily allow for Shari'ati's (1980, 1986) work on Islam and economic revolution to be incorporated. Likewise, a course on Durkheim could compare his views on the production of group collective consciousness (Durkheim 2008 [1912]) with Du Bois' (2008 [1920]) views on the production of the 'deep whiteness' shared by Europeans in the colonial world order – an analysis Karen Fields (2002) offers in her review of the two thinkers. Alternatively, a course could contrast the colonial ethnography of Durkheim and its presentation of indigenous people with the work of those using similar methods, but forming more critical perspectives – such as Kenyatta's (1979 [1938]) work with the Gikuyu people, where they are analysed *not* as pre-modern, but as having a highly structured, complex social life that was devastated by colonial rule.

3. Look for links even if you were not taught them yourself

In order to put traditionally 'canonical' authors into conversation with the wider circulation of ideas and themes, we need to collectively search for and find links between theorists and theories. Of course, this requires a significant amount of labour in some cases. Once we have a canon, and a way of framing and teaching that canon (such as with Marx, Weber and Durkheim separated from their colonial worlds), it becomes incredibly difficult to change the way that we collectively practise sociology. Across the generations, this canon is treated as being the sociological gospel; it is taught from professors to students; those students then become professors and teach it to their students; and so on. In this frame, reproduction becomes perfunctory, and the canon becomes common sense. For this reason, looking for epistemic and material links becomes a difficult task, especially for many of the teachers not versed in decolonial work who teach canonical sociology; but it is a task that we must collectively engage with in order to sustain a more critical sociology.

Take, for instance, Bourdieu and Foucault, whose work we analysed in the previous chapter. Both of these thinkers are often presented as being involved in metropolitan debates over metropolitan societies, such as the struggle between French Marxists, structuralists and existentialists.[30] Such presentations of these thinkers allow them to be construed as 'Northern theorists' who ignore colonialism and its effects in their work (Connell 2006; Saïd 1989). Bourdieu's time in Algeria is seen as an empirical backdrop for the formation of his concepts of habitus, field and capital, rather than being the context in which Bourdieu engaged with the works of Fanon and anti-colonialism.[31] Similarly, Foucault's links to Tunisian and Iranian anti-imperialism appear notably absent in accounts of his 'political turn' and shift towards analysing networks of power, *despite Foucault himself claiming the centrality of such experiences to his social thought.*[32] A decolonial practice of sociology does not ignore these links in the classroom, textbooks and journal articles, but uses these links as the foundation upon which we can build more transnational, critical analyses of various social processes.

The possibilities of these links are endless, finding inspiration not just from historical investigation but also from sociological creativity. Thus, historically we have already noted the link between Marx and Du Bois, but it is also worthwhile to consider Du Bois' admiration of Weber, and Weber's admiration of Du Bois[33] – there are empirical links here that can be teased out in terms of how the holy trinity of sociology are presented. In terms of creativity, building links between theories and theorists is about finding some kind of theoretical or empirical hook that allows us to put certain systems of ideas into conversation with one another – such as putting Gramsci's concepts of the subaltern and hegemony into conversation with Fanon's work on colonial violence, to understand life in the postcolony (Salem 2020), or putting Bourdieu's field theory into conversation with C. L. R. James' work on colonial insurgency, to understand how a revolution of enslaved people in one part of the world (as with Haiti) was capable of creating shifts across the whole colonial-imperial field (Go 2008, 2016a). Building links, therefore, is a critical way of developing our sociological imagination. They do not necessitate *using* Northern theory (e.g. Gramsci's concept of hegemony) to explain a reality in the South (life in the postcolony), but instead involve a *horizontal* conversation between different sociological approaches. This directly feeds into the next point.

4. Value the Global South regardless of Northern valuation schemes

This point means two things in particular. Firstly, there is the issue that we ought not to assume that all theory comes from the North, and the South can only be used as an empirical pool of data (Connell et al. 2018; Hountondji 1997). Indeed, while the idea that the colonies were 'pools' of data reverberated around the time of classical sociology (Keller 1906), this epistemic divide between Western theory and Southern data continues today through the practice of intellectual imperialism.[34] Challenging this epistemic inequality meaning-fully interrelates with all of the aforementioned points. There is no use in 'building links' between systems of ideas if we are *only* searching for people who have applied a 'Northern theory' to a Southern context (as, for instance, Heleieth Saffioti presciently did with using Marxism for feminist analysis in Brazil[35]). While such deployments of Western theory in Southern contexts are often appropriate, valuing the Global South regardless of Northern valuation schemes implies that we do not only value work from the Global South if it 'proves' or 'extends' a Western theory in a particular way. We thus need to also acknowledge the vast array of theory coming from the South itself, which was, from my reading, the main task of Connell's (2007a) *Southern Theory*.

Indeed, this also flows in another direction: we ought not to only value Southern theory (or theories) if it helps us to understand something in the West. As Connell (2010, 2018) argues, if we only value Southern theory in terms of the question 'What can the West gain from this?', then we simply reproduce the structure of the political economy of knowledge that decolonial sociology seeks to displace. Thus, Shari'ati's (1980) insights about the revolutionary teachings of Shi'a Islam may develop Western Marxism, humanism and existentialism, but his work is not only valuable because of these contributions. Similarly, Ibn Khaldūn's work on social solidarity (asabiyya) and societal change is valuable not just because it enables us to counter Marx or Weber's framing of the 'Asiatic world' as being static, but because it stands as a theory in itself.

5. Do not 'neoliberalize' decolonial work

There is a kind of marketized logic in the idea that we ought to only value Southern knowledge if it benefits the West, or Western theory. Value is defined in terms of a certain form of productivity – in this case, the productivity being expansion of Western theory or understanding of certain social phenomena in the West. Knowledge, in this sense, becomes tied to the concept of usefulness. This valuation scheme ties directly into debates over knowledge production in neoliberal universities.[36]

Student-led social movements such as 'Rhodes Must Fall' at the University of Cape Town, University of Oxford and Harvard University demonstrate a growing global cognizance that universities are deeply embedded in the logic of coloniality.[37] However, at the very same time, as pinpointed by Ahmed (2015) and Connell (2019), universities are now also increasingly cognizant that they can use 'decolonizing the curriculum', or 'decolonizing the university', as marketing signals within their wider diversity regimes. Universities across the world are thus transforming 'decolonization' into a profit scheme, consequently truncating the potential for such radical decolonial work within these institutions to begin with.

Indeed, as Bacevic (2019) shows, part of the reason why such critical work decreases is because academics themselves come to internalize the market-based logic of neoliberalism. This market-based logic encourages academics to measure their value in terms of productivity, scholarly outputs, fellowships, prestigious manuscripts and so on. This leads to a situation where, as Bacevic (2019: 389) describes:

The type of energy and effort that could be invested into, for instance, the sustained organization and/or mobilization of labour against neoliberal transformations, goes instead into the organisation of public lectures, roundtables, or 'chasing' publications [...] screaming 'fuck neoliberalism' into the safe confines of journal articles or social media – while, undeniably, important as a mobilising force – is hardly sufficient to undo multiple infrastructural, political, and other inequalities, including those that are reproduced through the same venues.

Drawing a parallel between Bacevic's comment and decolonialism, there is a firm difference between writing and shouting about decolonialism in academic publications and colloquia, and creating conditions for a decolonial world to arise and be sustained in the first place. To clarify with an example, many of us in British academia are now writing about decolonialism – broadly, and also within sociology. However, Britain is also structured such that our visa laws pretty much restrict visiting academics from the Global South from attending (and thus keynoting or presenting at) British conference colloquia.[38] Writing about and discussing 'decolonizing sociology' is thus an important step, but it counts for very little if we are still working in a country that excludes, and denies any meaningful dialogue with and presence of, academics in the Global South at key conferences.

It thus becomes important for those of us doing decolonial work to measure our contributions not solely through marketized models of valuation, but also in terms of the work we are doing to 'undo those multiple infrastructural, political, and other inequalities' (Bacevic 2019: 389) produced through coloniality. This feeds into the wider point that 'decolonizing sociology' is much more than a scholastic activity. Rather, we work towards a decolonial sociology not just because we want to make sociology more critical, or 'better', but also because we want epistemic justice (Santos 2014). Decolonial thinking holds that when we devalue certain systems of thought, this is inseparable from devaluing the *people* who produce and live by these systems of thought (Mignolo 2002). Decolonizing sociology, therefore, is not just a scholastic activity that can be measured by neoliberal metrics; through decolonizing the discipline we can strengthen the mission of epistemic justice, and thus speak back to the global system of coloniality that devalues the being of certain people. Within sociology, this becomes difficult, given linguistic layers of exclusion in the global political economy of knowledge.

6. Encourage students and scholars to be multilingual

Most, if not all, of the major sociology journals are published in English. This means that scholars around the world, regardless of their first language, if they want to fulfil the neoliberal criteria of publishing in 'top' journals, must be fluent in reading and writing English.[39] This is already an issue of coloniality, but we can problematize it even further. Namely, who gets to be translated into English? This broadly highlights the social problem around which authors, and which ideas, get introduced to the sociological community. Thus, the fact that Bourdieu wrote in French has not been a significant barrier to his international reputation (see Lamont 2012) – a significant amount of his oeuvre is either published in English or being translated into English. However, the same cannot be said for many other sociologists writing in non-English languages – often coming from the modernity/ coloniality paradigms, such as Aníbal Quijano, Heleieth Saffioti and Gino Germani, to name just three. There is a copious amount of critical work in sociology that gets invisiblized through an epistemicide that has rendered English a universal language for academic knowledge production. Many authors writing in non-English languages thus rely on the whim of publishers to be translated. Given that the decision to translate certain works itself relies on certain valuation systems, we can see how the hegemony of the Global North over the South thus creates particular problems for non-English writers in the Global South being 'translated to' Western audiences.

Indeed, this issue of English-centrism is one reason why Anzaldúa (1987) deliberately slips between multiple languages in her writing – to unsettle the comfort of belonging in, and valuing, one particular language. As Anzaldúa (2009: 26–7) states in 'Speaking in Tongues':

> Because white eyes do not want to know us, they do not bother to learn our language, the language which reflects us, our culture, our spirit. [...] And though now I write my poems in Spanish as well as English I feel the rip-off of my native tongue.

In Anzaldúa's comment we can see a clear link between valuation and translation. Lots of critical work goes untranslated into English because the English-speaking audience 'do not want to know us'. While it is not the job solely of the sociologist, we must still collectively be cognizant of ongoing linguistic systems of exclusion, and universities where this is a problem ought to be addressing this as a key issue in decolonial practice.

7. Accept that decolonizing sociology does not have a finishing point

Talk of 'decolonizing sociology' seems to imply that 'sociology' is a phenomenon that can itself become 'decolonized'. This would mean that there is a specific end point for decolonizing sociology, a specific moment when we can collectively agree that the discipline has become decolonized and the mission has been achieved. This kind of reading makes us think that by restructuring the way we teach certain courses – such as Marxism – or by situating the canon and discipline in their imperial roots, the work is done and we can collectively move on. However, it is much more apt to see 'decolonizing sociology' as an approach rather than an achievable goal. Not only does this save us from any sense of complacency, but it also reminds us that the decolonial links we can draw and form in sociology are endless, so long as we retain an open sociological imagination. Furthermore, seeing decolonizing sociology as something that can be achieved and then moved on from provides a very mistaken account of how academic disciplines work in the first place.

Throughout this book we have tended towards discussing 'sociology' as if it is a unified house in need of decolonization, but this is far from the truth. Sociology is like every other discipline in the way that there is infighting over who the canonical authors are, what the correct way of doing sociology is, what the boundaries of sociology are; and, indeed, there is even more infighting once we look at the various subfields within the larger field of sociology – whether that be cultural sociology, economic sociology, political sociology and so on. To many people, decolonial sociology is just this – a subfield within the larger field of sociology, a specific way of doing sociology that has its own relatively autonomous valuation scheme from the rest of the field. This could, indeed, be true, and there is evidence for seeing decolonial sociology as a subfield within the overall discipline.[40]

However, there is a central difference that decolonial sociology, as a subfield, has from other subfields in sociology. Subfields such as cultural sociology, political sociology, economic sociology and so on recognize themselves as subfields. On the other hand, decolonial sociology may recognize itself as a subfield, but it equally well sees itself as struggling for control over the total field of sociology – with its goal being to restructure the sociological field and its systems and practices of (e)valuation. If decolonial sociology did manage to reshape the sociological field in this way – cognizant of its imperial origins, making it more open to connections and links, rejecting bifurcation and Orientalism, built on horizontal conversation between different traditions, and so on – the work of 'decolonizing sociology' would still not be achieved. This is because there would still be tensions within the field from those who want to restructure this newly designed field. In other words, decolonial sociology would still need to constantly, actively maintain its vision of the discipline in order for that vision to be extended throughout time.

A long way forward, but with a long road behind

This aim of decolonial sociology, to restructure the field of sociology itself, seems a daunting task. Hopefully, through reading this book, you can see why embracing a decolonial option in sociology seems the most apt course of action, not just for the sake of deepening the analytical faculties of sociology, but also for the sake of striving for epistemic justice and equality. However, hopefully, through reading this book, you are also aware that as daunting as this task is, there are centuries of thinkers who themselves constructed this road on which we are now having our discussion about sociology and decoloniality.

In Māori epistemology, 'it is impossible to conceive of the present and the future as separate and distinct from the past, for the past is constitutive of the present and, as such, is inherently reconstituted within the future' (Stewart-Harawira 2005: 42). This statement does not just echo in sociology's entanglements with colonialism, and its internalization and reproduction of the colonial episteme in the present day. The idea that the past is inherently reconstituted in the future also applies when thinking about those past thinkers who have opened up the road, and enabled us to think about decolonialism within sociology today. There is a plethora of critical, sociological work that took place outside of the colonial episteme, and any attempt to have a 'decolonial revolution' in sociology in the future requires engagement with and valuation of such past work.

This takes us back to the opening theme of this chapter – decoloniality as an option. In sociology, decoloniality implies situating the development of sociology in its colonial origins in order to better understand its Eurocentric logic today, rejecting the idea that we can build universal social theories based on provincial, bifurcated accounts of the West, interrogating Southern standpoints which expand the scope of sociology beyond its current limitations, looking beyond mainstream methodologies which constrain the reach of sociological knowledge, and building horizontal conversations between different sociological traditions. Decoloniality in sociology, therefore, is an option which needs to be embraced not just to deepen the analytical capabilities of the discipline, but also in order to support the wider project of global epistemic justice. In this book I have attempted to show how this question of decoloniality and epistemic justice has been framed within sociology, the various approaches that have been taken to instigate this cognitive justice, and the ways that this epistemic equality is essential for forming critical analyses of social phenomena. The question now turns to you, and whether you wish to embrace the decolonial option, and collectively, as a sociological community, whether we can work to restructure the discipline to make it more equitable on a global level. Sustaining this decolonial movement in sociology may be difficult, but it cannot be deferred to future sociological generations. As the proverb goes:

Don't delay today's work until tomorrow.

Notes

Introduction

1 Furthermore, even the invention of 'Indian' and indigenous as a social category is a good example of how colonialism had ontological effects, as here we see lots of different indigenous people being reduced to one identification, having previously seen themselves as disparate (Mignolo 2011a).

2 See Bourdieu 2004; Collins 1998; Harding 2004. References throughout this book often appear in endnotes. When thinkers are typically associated with a particular point of view, concept or argument, efforts have been made to include them as in-text citations.

3 For instance Alatas and Sinha 2001; Domingues 2009.

4 As discussed in Bhambra 2007; Boatcă et al. 2010; Connell 1997, 2007a; Go 2013a, 2014, 2016a; Steinmetz 2013.

5 See Claeys (2010) for a discussion of Comte's opposition to British imperialism.

6 For instance, as presented in Holmwood and Scott 2014; Scott 2010.

7 See Go 2011; Hall 1992.

8 Alatas and Sinha 2001, 2017; Morrison 1995.

9 A journal founded by Durkheim himself in 1898.

10 See Go 2014.

11 As argued by Small 1906; Thomas 1896; Vincent 1896; Ward 1895.

12 See Mills 1997.

13 See Lewis 2012; Carey 2011.

14 Several papers on this issue have been published, including Go 2018; Magubane 2016; Meer 2018.

15 The first recorded use of the term 'sociology' in the US, for instance, was in Fitzhugh's (1854) *Sociology for the South*, where he argued that enforcing enslavement in the US South was important to maintain the country's morality. Other contemporaries of Du Bois and Frazier, such as John Crozier, Howard Odum and Charles Ellwood, all argued that Black US Americans were unable to assimilate into the country due to their blood-born inferiority, with Crozier and Odum using this as justification for segregating Black US Americans (Frazier 1947; see also Magubane 2013).

16 Indeed, Du Bois was interested in wider processes of enslavement, imperialism, colonialism and empire, and throughout this book we will focus on Du Bois' decolonial sociology. However, such decolonial work was not pursued in the Atlanta Laboratory studies, which retained an exclusive focus on American inner cities (Wright 2002a, 2016).

1. The Decolonial Challenge to Sociology

1 See Meghji 2019a.
2 See also Connell 2007a, 2007b.
3 See also Alatas and Sinha 2001, 2017; Dussel 1999; Patel 2014.
4 Such as in Delacroix's *Women of Algiers in Their Apartment* (see Kuehn 2011).
5 Such as in Joy's *The Death of General Gordon* (see Ali 2015).
6 See Fryer 1984; Hall 1992.
7 See Alatas 1993; Hall 1992.
8 See Alatas and Sinha 2001; Turner 1974, 1978, 1989.
9 See Ince 2012; Palacios 2002.
10 As argued in Césaire 2001 [1950] and Wolfe 2006.
11 For ethical reasons, I have redacted the 'N word' from this quote.
12 It is perhaps worth mentioning that Bourdieu, unlike the other sociologists mentioned by Connell in this quote, did actually engage with anti-colonialism, and consequently with 'Southern realities' (see Go 2013b; Puwar 2009; Steinmetz 2009; Yacine 2016). We will discuss this relationship in chapter 3.
13 See Young 2004.
14 See also Myoung-Kyu and Kyung-Sup 1999.

15 See also Slabodsky 2010, 2016.
16 The term favoured in Buchholz 2016; Go 2008, 2011; Steinmetz 2008.
17 The term favoured in Amin 1991; Dussel 1999, 2002; Quijano and Wallerstein 1992.
18 It is also worth pointing out that other sociologists have referred to the same premise as 'modernity/coloniality' with other terms, such as with Patel's (2017) notion of 'colonial modernity'.
19 See Meghji 2017a; Solomos 2014.
20 See Rabaka 2009 for an analysis of this intellectual history.
21 See Virdee 2017 for a further analysis of anti-imperial 'second sight'.
22 For instance, Bhambra 2007; Du Bois 2007 [1947], 2012 [1920]; Dubois 2004; Go 2016a; Hammer and White 2018; James 2001 [1938].
23 For an analysis of contemporary French republicanism, see Beaman 2017.
24 See Du Bois 2007 [1947]).
25 See Du Bois 2007 [1947], 2012 [1920]; Dubois 2004; Go 2016a; James 2001 [1938])
26 See Du Bois 2007 [1947]; Gopal 2019.
27 In terms of history, this would also be important to the development of sociology. Du Bois pioneered ethnographic empirical sociology in his *Philadelphia Negro* (1967 [1899]) and his work at the Atlanta School (see Wright 2002a) in the 1890s. Kenyatta's intervention would thus be occurring in 1938 – around the same time that ethnographic sociology takes off at the Chicago School (Wright 2012). Centring the Chicago School as the beginning of empirical sociology thus overlooks not only Du Boisian contributions which happened earlier, but also work such as that by Kenyatta (1979 [1938]) that occurred concurrently. It is also worth noting that Kenyatta is a writer who develops social theory while simultaneously being an anti-colonial activist – thus falling into what Go (2016a) and Shari'ati (1986) envisage as the 'first wave' of de/postcolonial scholars who were all scholar activists.
28 This relates to Césaire's (2001 [1950]) boomerang theory, where he argues that in attempting to implement democracy in their colonies, those in the metropoles simply dehumanized and de-democratized *themselves* (see also Sarkar 1912).

2. Beyond Intellectual Imperialism

1 See Meller 1989; Steinmetz 1997.
2 See Connell et al. 2018; Maia 2014.
3 See Connell et al. 2017, 2018.
4 Indeed, this is true of Latin America as a whole, with chairs in sociology being appointed in 'Bogotá 1882, Asuncion 1900, Quito 1906 and Mexico 1907' (Pereyra 2010: 213).
5 See Coetzee 2008; Uys 2010.
6 Dufoix 2018; Patel 2010.
7 See Dufoix 2018; Sall and Ouedraogo 2010; Steinmetz 2013.
8 See Chang 2002; Grosfoguel 2007.
9 On canon formation in theory, see Outhwaite 2009.
10 https://www.elsevier.com/connect/11–steps-to-structuring-a-science-paper-editors-will-take-seriously.
11 See Alatas 2010; Maia 2014.
12 It should be noted that Cabral (1966) makes a similar point in exposing the limitations of classical Marxism in 'The Weapon of Theory', when he states that: 'Those who affirm – in our case correctly – that the motive force of history is the class struggle would certainly agree to a revision of this affirmation to make it more precise and give it an even wider field of application if they had a better knowledge of the essential characteristics of certain colonized peoples, that is to say peoples dominated by imperialism.'
13 As argued by Dufoix 2018.

3. Walking while Asking Questions

1 As well as social movements such as the Black Panther Party and the Combahee River Collective.
2 See Itzigsohn and Brown 2020; Morris 2017; Wright 2016.
3 See Wright 2002a, 2002b, 2012, 2016; Wright and Calhoun 2012.
4 See Itzigsohn and Brown 2020.
5 The material Du Bois collected through such travels is collated in his *Black Folk: Then and Now* (Du Bois 2007 [1896]).
6 See also Meghji 2017b.
7 See also Leonardo 2002.

8   Bhambra 2007; Go 2016a; Williams 1944.
9   See Roediger 2017.
10 See also Lipsitz 1998.
11 The zone of non-being is also summarized in Ciccariello-Maher 2010; Gordon 2007; Tinsley 2019.
12 See Butler 2006. It is also worth noting that Sartre wrote prefaces to editions of Fanon's *The Wretched of the Earth* and *Black Skin, White Masks*, while Fanon (2008 [1952]) argued that Sartre helped him to see the links between anti-Semitism and anti-Blackness.
13 See Salem 2020; Zeiny 2017.
14 This meant that Shari'ati also positioned himself against the sociology of Weber, who saw Islam as anti-modern (Shari'ati 1986; Turner 1974, 1978).
15 Religious sociology is being posited here rather than a 'sociology of religion', as religion is not just the object of sociological study, but the method of sociologizing in the first place.
16 On coloniality and the development of French social theory, see Ahluwalia 2010; Burawoy 2019; Go 2013b; Puwar 2009; Yacine 2016.
17 See Go 2013b.
18 Go 2013b; Yacine 2016.
19 Ahluwalia 2010; Medien 2019.
20 Afary and Anderson 2010.
21 Puwar 2009.
22 Go 2013b; Steinmetz 2017.
23 See Meghji 2019b; Puwar 2009; Wallace 2017.
24 See Bourdieu 1977, 1990a; Bourdieu and Wacquant 1992; Wacquant and Akçaoğlu 2017.
25 Go 2013b; Steinmetz 2017.
26 For instance, Bourdieu 1961 [1958], 1979 [1963]; Bourdieu and Sayad 2018 [1964].
27 See Wacquant 2008.
28 For example, Connell 2006, 2007a, 2018; Saïd 1989.
29 See Baert and Carreira da Silva 2009; Gutting 2005; McNay 2013; Medien 2019; Mills 2003.

Conclusion

1   See also Harding 1991, 2004.
2   See also Bonilla-Silva 2017; Frazier 1947; Meghji 2019a.

3 See also Collins 2000, 2019.
4 As per the Du Boisian approach to sociology (see Du Bois 1968, 2007 [1940], 2012 [1920]).
5 Wainwright 2011.
6 And, of course, it is worth pointing out that the destruction of the environment was not always performed simply through land and resource expropriation; the genocide of indigenous Americans, for instance, contributed to a global cooling that created a mini 'ice age' (see Koch et al. 2019).
7 See Sealey-Huggins 2017, 2018.
8 As reported by Sanderson 2019.
9 As reported by Lamble 2013.
10 Bhattacharyya 2018; Sealey-Huggins 2017, 2018.
11 See Figueroa Helland and Lindgren 2016; Whyte 2017, 2018.
12 As we see currently, with Brazilian President Bolsonaro's 2018 presidential campaign including a key policy agenda to expropriate more indigenous land for oil sales and private profit.
13 Indeed, this also has similarities with the social thought of Indian sociologist Benoy Kumar Sarkar (1912: 13), who argues that the 'physical universe is not only the feeder and sustainer of living beings, it is also the abode in which they grow and reproduce themselves. Hence the action and reaction between the living organism and the environment regulate all conditions of its life-history.'
14 Denzin 1997, 2017.
15 Zuberi 2000, 2001; Zuberi and Bonilla-Silva 2008.
16 See Angosto-Ferrández 2014; Loveman 2009a, 2009b, 2014; Loveman et al. 2012; Saldívar and Walsh 2014.
17 On settler colonialism, see Kauanui 2016.
18 Of course, these nations are just two of many possible examples.
19 Reviewed in works such as Denzin et al. 2008; Kovach 2010; Smith 2008 [1999].
20 Carreira da Silva 2016; Connell 1997; Lamont 2009; Outhwaite 2009.
21 Bourdieu 2004.
22 Tuck and Yang 2012.
23 And for this reason, many of these points speak directly to sociologists working in the West.
24 Connell et al. 2018.
25 See Go 2016a for a critique of Mann's bifurcation.
26 Tinsley 2019.
27 See Bhambra 2007, 2014; Bhambra and Santos 2017.

28 As summarized in Alatas and Sinha 2001; Bhambra 2007.

29 Of course, the emphasis here is on the central features of the authors' canonical works. Revisionists such as Anderson (2010), for instance, have shed light on some of Marx's footnotes, comments and journalistic writings where he argues that colonialism allowed European nations to gain maximum profits, while Karen Fields (2002) has pointed out that Durkheim dedicated some time to discussing anti-Semitism in the context of European imperialism, and Scaff (1998) and Chandler (2006) have both pointed out that through correspondence with Du Bois, Weber did see the racialized components of capitalist economies.

30 See Baert and Carreira da Silva 2009; Jenkins 2014; Mills 2003; Swartz 1997.

31 See Puwar 2009.

32 See Medien 2019.

33 As reviewed in Hughey and Goss 2018.

34 On intellectual imperialism, see Alatas 2000; Gareau 1988; Hountondji 1997; Onwuzuruigbo 2018.

35 See Connell 2015; Pinto 2014 for a review of Saffioti's work.

36 On neoliberalism and education see Bacevic 2019.

37 On these student-led social movements, see Bhambra et al. 2018; Connell et al. 2017; Mbembe 2016.

38 As reported by Grant 2019.

39 Indeed, many of us in the West are bilingual in virtue of family trajectories, and, as clarified under this point, many sociologists across the world (and in the Global South in particular) are bilingual in virtue of global English-centrism. This point speaks more broadly to the structure of academia and the politics of translation.

40 Largely because ghettoizing decolonial work into a subfield allows those debates to happen internally to decolonial scholars, rather than reaching out to those who can ignore these discussions as they define themselves broadly as 'political sociologists', 'cultural sociologists' and so on (Virdee 2019).

References

Adésínà, Jìmí O. 2006. 'Sociology Beyond Despair: Recovery of Nerve, Endogeneity, and Epistemic Intervention'. *South African Review of Sociology* 37 (2): 241–59.

Afary, Janet, and Kevin B. Anderson. 2010. *Foucault and the Iranian Revolution: Gender and the Seductions of Islamism.* Chicago, IL: University of Chicago Press.

Ahluwalia, Pal. 2010. 'Post-Structuralism's Colonial Roots: Michel Foucault'. *Social Identities* 16 (5): 597–606.

Ahmed, Sara. 2006. *Queer Phenomenology: Orientations, Objects, Others.* Durham, NC: Duke University Press.

Ahmed, Sara. 2015. 'Doing Diversity Work in Higher Education'. In *Aiming Higher: Race, Inequality and Diversity in the Academy,* edited by Claire Alexander and Jason Arday, 6–7. London: Runnymede Trust.

Akiwowo, Akinsola. 1986. 'Contributions to the Sociology of Knowledge from an African Oral Poetry'. *International Sociology* 1 (4): 343–58.

Akiwowo, Akinsola. 1999. 'Indigenous Sociologies: Extending the Scope of the Argument'. *International Sociology* 14 (2): 115–38.

Alatas, Syed Farid. 1993. 'A Khaldūnian Perspective on the Dynamics of Asiatic Societies'. *Comparative Civilizations Review* 29: 29–51.

Alatas, Syed Farid. 2000. 'An Introduction to the Idea of Alternative Discourses'. *Southeast Asian Journal of Social Science* 28 (1): 1–12.

Alatas, Syed Farid. 2003. 'Academic Dependency and the Global Division of Labour in the Social Sciences'. *Current Sociology* 51 (6): 599–613.

Alatas, Syed Farid. 2010. 'Religion and Reform: Two Exemplars for Autonomous Sociology in the Non-Western Context'. In *The ISA Handbook of Diverse Sociological Traditions*, edited by Sujata Patel, 29–39. Los Angeles, CA: SAGE.

Alatas, Syed Farid. 2014. *Applying Ibn Khaldūn: The Recovery of a Lost Tradition in Sociology*. New York, NY: Routledge.

Alatas, Syed Farid, and Vineeta Sinha. 2001. 'Teaching Classical Sociological Theory in Singapore: The Context of Eurocentrism'. *Teaching Sociology* 29 (3): 316–31.

Alatas, Syed Farid, and Vineeta Sinha. 2017. *Sociological Theory Beyond the Canon*. London: Palgrave.

Alatas, Syed Hussein. 2000. 'Intellectual Imperialism: Definition, Traits, and Problems'. *Southeast Asian Journal of Social Science* 28 (1): 23–45.

Alatas, Syed Hussein. 2002. 'The Development of an Autonomous Social Science Tradition in Asia: Problems and Prospects'. *Asian Journal of Social Science* 30 (1): 150–7.

Alatas, Syed Hussein. 2006. 'The Autonomous, the Universal and the Future of Sociology'. *Current Sociology* 54 (1): 7–23.

Alatas, Syed Hussein. 2013 [1977]. *The Myth of the Lazy Native: A Study of the Image of the Malays, Filipinos and Javanese from the 16th to the 20th Century and Its Function in the Ideology of Colonial Capitalism*. New York, NY: Routledge.

Ali, Isra. 2015. 'The Harem Fantasy in Nineteenth-Century Orientalist Paintings'. *Dialectical Anthropology* 39 (1): 33–46.

Amin, Samir. 1991. 'The Ancient World-Systems versus the Modern Capitalist World-System'. *Review (Fernand Braudel Center)* 14 (3): 349–85.

Amster, Ellen J. 2013. *Medicine and the Saints: Science, Islam, and the Colonial Encounter in Morocco, 1877–1956*. Austin, TX: University of Texas Press.

Anderson, Kevin B. 2010. *Marx at the Margins: On Nationalism, Ethnicity, and Non-Western Societies.* Chicago, IL: University of Chicago Press.

Angosto-Ferrández, Luis F. 2014. 'From "Café Con Leche" to "o Café, o Leche": National Identity, Mestizaje and Census Politics in Contemporary Venezuela'. *Journal of Iberian and Latin American Research* 20 (3): 373–98.

Anzaldúa, Gloria. 1987. *Borderlands/La Frontera: The New Mestiza.* San Francisco, CA: Aunt Lute Books.

Anzaldúa, Gloria. 2006 [1987]. 'To Live in the Borderlands Means You'. In *American Identities: An Introductory Textbook*, edited by Lois P. Rudnick, Judith E. Smith and Rachel Lee Rubin, 316–17. Malden, MA: Blackwell.

Anzaldúa, Gloria. 2009. 'Speaking in Tongues'. In *The Gloria Anzladúa Reader*, edited by AnaLouise Keating, 26–35. Durham, NC: Duke University Press.

Archer, Margaret Scotford. 2003. *Structure, Agency and the Internal Conversation.* Cambridge: Cambridge University Press.

Arjomand, Saïd Amir. 2008. 'Southern Theory: An Illusion'. *European Journal of Sociology/Archives Européennes de Sociologie/Europäisches Archiv für Soziologie* 49 (3): 546–9.

Azarya, Victor. 2010. 'Academic Excellence and Social Relevance: Israeli Sociology in Universities and Beyond'. In *The ISA Handbook of Diverse Sociological Traditions*, edited by Sujata Patel, 246–56. Los Angeles, CA: SAGE.

Bacevic, Jana. 2019. 'Knowing Neoliberalism'. *Social Epistemology* Online First.

Baert, Patrick, and Filipe Carreira da Silva. 2009. *Social Theory in the Twentieth Century and Beyond.* 2nd edn. Cambridge: Polity.

Banton, Michael, and Jonathan Harwood. 1975. *The Race Concept.* Newton Abbot: David & Charles.

Barnes, Harry E. 1919. 'The Struggle of Races and Social Groups as a Factor in the Development of Political and Social Institutions: An Exposition and Critique of the Sociological System of Ludwig Gumplowicz'. *The Journal of Race Development* 9 (4): 394–419.

Beaman, Jean. 2017. *Citizen Outsider: Children of North African Immigrants in France*. Berkeley, CA: University of California Press.

Beck, Ulrich. 1992. *Risk Society: Towards a New Modernity*. London: SAGE.

Beck, Ulrich. 2000. *What Is Globalization?* Oxford: Blackwell.

Beck, Ulrich. 2002. *Individualization: Institutionalized Individualism and Its Social and Political Consequences*. London: SAGE.

Bhabha, Homi. 1994. *The Location of Culture*. London: Routledge.

Bhambra, Gurminder K. 2007. *Rethinking Modernity: Postcolonialism and the Sociological Imagination*. London: Palgrave Macmillan.

Bhambra, Gurminder K. 2010. 'Sociology after Postcolonialism: Provincialized Cosmopolitanisms and Connected Sociologies'. In *Decolonizing European Sociology: Transdisciplinary Approaches*, edited by Manuela Boatcă, Sérgio Costa and Encarnacion Gutierrez Rodriguez, 33–47. Farnham: Ashgate.

Bhambra, Gurminder K. 2014. *Connected Sociologies*. London: Bloomsbury.

Bhambra, Gurminder K. 2020. 'Introduction – Roots, Routes, and Reconstruction: Travelling Ideas/Theories'. *The Sociological Review* 68 (3): 455–60.

Bhambra, Gurminder K., Dalia Gebrial and Kerem Nişancıoğlu. 2018. *Decolonising the University*. London: Pluto Press.

Bhambra, Gurminder K., and Boaventura de Sousa Santos. 2017. 'Introduction: Global Challenges for Sociology'. *Sociology* 51 (1): 3–10.

Bhattacharyya, Gargi. 2018. *Rethinking Racial Capitalism: Questions of Reproduction and Survival*. Lanham, MD: Rowman & Littlefield.

Boatcă, Manuela, Sérgio Costa and Encarnacion Gutierrez Rodriguez. 2010. 'Introduction: Decolonizing European Sociology: Different Paths Towards a Pending Project'. In *Decolonizing European Sociology: Transdisciplinary*

Approaches, edited by Manuela Boatcǎ, Sérgio Costa and Encarnacion Gutierrez Rodriguez, 1–10. Farnham: Ashgate.

Bonilla-Silva, Eduardo. 2015. 'More than Prejudice: Restatement, Reflections, and New Directions in Critical Race Theory'. *Sociology of Race and Ethnicity* 1 (1): 73–87.

Bonilla-Silva, Eduardo. 2017. 'What We Were, What We Are, and What We Should Be: The Racial Problem of American Sociology'. *Social Problems* 64 (2): 179–87.

Bonilla-Silva, Eduardo, and Tukufu Zuberi. 2008. 'Towards a Definition of White Logic and White Methods'. In *White Logic, White Methods*, edited by Tukufu Zuberi and Eduardo Bonilla-Silva, 3–27. Lanham, MD: Rowman & Littlefield.

Bourdieu, Pierre. 1961 [1958]. *The Algerians*. Boston, MA: Beacon Press.

Bourdieu, Pierre. 1977. *Outline of a Theory of Practice*. Cambridge: Cambridge University Press.

Bourdieu, Pierre. 1979 [1963]. *Algeria 1960*. Cambridge: Cambridge University Press.

Bourdieu, Pierre. 1990a. *The Logic of Practice*. Cambridge: Polity.

Bourdieu, Pierre. 1990b. *In Other Words: Essays Towards a Reflexive Sociology*. Stanford, CA: Stanford University Press.

Bourdieu, Pierre. 1998. *Practical Reason: On the Theory of Action*. Cambridge: Polity.

Bourdieu, Pierre. 2000. *Pascalian Meditations*. Stanford, CA: Stanford University Press.

Bourdieu, Pierre. 2004. *Science of Science and Reflexivity*. Cambridge: Polity.

Bourdieu, Pierre. 2008. *Sketch for a Self-Analysis*. Chicago, IL: University of Chicago Press.

Bourdieu, Pierre. 2010 [1979]. *Distinction: A Social Critique of the Judgement of Taste*. Abingdon: Routledge.

Bourdieu, Pierre, and Jean-Claude Passeron. 1990. *Reproduction in Education, Society and Culture*. Translated by Richard Nice. 2nd edn. London: SAGE.

Bourdieu, Pierre, and Abdelmalek Sayad. 2018 [1964]. *The Crisis of Traditional Agriculture in Algeria*. Cambridge: Polity.

Bourdieu, Pierre, and Loïc Wacquant. 1992. *An Invitation to Reflexive Sociology*. Cambridge: Polity.

Briceño-León, Roberto. 2010. 'The Five Dilemmas of Latin American Sociology'. In *The ISA Handbook of Diverse Sociological Traditions*, edited by Sujata Patel, 177–88. Los Angeles, CA: SAGE.

Bringel, Breno, and José Maurício Domingues. 2017. 'Social Theory, Extroversion and Autonomy: Dilemmas of Contemporary (Semi) Peripheral Sociology'. *Méthod(e)s: African Review of Social Sciences Methodology* 2 (1–2): 108–26.

Buchholz, Larissa. 2016. 'What Is a Global Field? Theorizing Fields beyond the Nation-State'. *The Sociological Review* 64 (2): 31–60.

Burawoy, Michael. 2010. 'Forging Global Sociology from Below'. In *The ISA Handbook of Diverse Sociological Traditions*, edited by Sujata Patel, 52–65. Los Angeles, CA: SAGE.

Burawoy, Michael. 2015. 'Facing an Unequal World: Challenges for a Global Sociology'. *Current Sociology* 63 (1): 5–34.

Burawoy, Michael. 2019. *Symbolic Violence: Conversations with Bourdieu*. Durham, NC: Duke University Press.

Butler, Judith. 2006. 'Violence, Non-Violence: Sartre on Fanon'. *Graduate Faculty Philosophy Journal* 27 (1): 3–24.

Cabral, Amílcar. 1966. 'The Weapon of Theory'. Tricontinental Conference of the Peoples of Asia, Africa and Latin America. Havana, Cuba.

Carey, Hilary M. 2011. *God's Empire: Religion and Colonialism in the British World, c.1801–1908*. Cambridge: Cambridge University Press.

Carreira da Silva, Filipe. 2016. 'Following the Book: Towards a Pragmatic Sociology of the Book'. *Sociology* 50 (6): 1185–200.

Cassano, Franco. 2010. 'South of Every North'. In

Decolonizing European Sociology: Transdisciplinary Approaches, edited by Manuela Boatcă, Sérgio Costa and Encarnacion Gutierrez Rodriguez, 213–24. Farnham: Ashgate.

Césaire, Aimé. 2001 [1950]. *Discourse on Colonialism*. New York, NY: NYU Press.

Chakrabarty, Dipesh. 2009a. *Provincializing Europe: Postcolonial Thought and Historical Difference – New Edition*. Princeton, NJ: Princeton University Press.

Chakrabarty, Dipesh. 2009b. 'The Climate of History: Four Theses'. *Critical Inquiry* 35 (2): 197–222.

Chandler, Nahum D. 2006. 'The Possible Form of an Interlocution: W. E. B. Du Bois and Max Weber in Correspondence, 1904–1905'. *CR: The New Centennial Review* 6 (3): 193–239.

Chang, Ha-Joon. 2002. *Kicking Away the Ladder: Development Strategy in Historical Perspective*. London: Anthem Press.

Chen, Hon-Fai. 2018. *Chinese Sociology: State-Building and the Institutionalization of Globally Circulated Knowledge*. London: Palgrave.

Ciccariello-Maher, George. 2010. 'Jumpstarting the Decolonial Engine: Symbolic Violence from Fanon to Chávez'. *Theory & Event* 13 (1).

Claeys, Gregory. 2010. *Imperial Sceptics: British Critics of Empire, 1850–1920*. Cambridge: Cambridge University Press.

Coetzee, J. M. 2008. 'The Mind of Apartheid: Geoffrey Cronjé (1907–)'. *Social Dynamics* 17 (1): 1–35.

Collins, Patricia Hill. 1986. 'Learning from the Outsider Within: The Sociological Significance of Black Feminist Thought'. *Social Problems* 33 (6): s14–32.

Collins, Patricia Hill. 1998. *Fighting Words: Black Women and the Search for Justice*. Minneapolis, MN: University of Minnesota Press.

Collins, Patricia Hill. 2000. *Black Feminist Thought: Knowledge, Consciousness, and the Politics of Empowerment*. New York, NY: Routledge.

Collins, Patricia Hill. 2004. *Black Sexual Politics: African*

Americans, Gender, and the New Racism. New York, NY: Routledge.

Collins, Patricia Hill. 2019. *Intersectionality as Critical Social Theory*. Durham, NC: Duke University Press.

Collins, Randall. 1981. 'On the Microfoundations of Macrosociology'. *American Journal of Sociology* 86 (5): 984–1014.

Collins, Randall. 1997. 'A Sociological Guilt Trip: Comment on Connell'. *American Journal of Sociology* 102 (6): 1558–64.

Comte, Auguste. 2009 [1853]. *The Positive Philosophy of Auguste Comte: Vol. 2*. Cambridge: Cambridge University Press.

Connell, Raewyn. 1997. 'Why Is Classical Theory Classical?' *American Journal of Sociology* 102 (6): 1511–57.

Connell, Raewyn. 2006. 'Northern Theory: The Political Geography of General Social Theory'. *Theory and Society* 35 (2): 237–64.

Connell, Raewyn. 2007a. *Southern Theory: The Global Dynamics of Knowledge in Social Science*. Cambridge: Polity.

Connell, Raewyn. 2007b. 'The Northern Theory of Globalization'. *Sociological Theory* 25 (4): 368–85.

Connell, Raewyn. 2010. 'Learning from Each Other: Sociology on a World Scale'. In *The ISA Handbook of Diverse Sociological Traditions*, edited by Sujata Patel, 40–51. Los Angeles, CA: SAGE.

Connell, Raewyn. 2011. 'Decolonizing European Sociology: Transdisciplinary Approaches'. *Contemporary Sociology* 40 (3): 341–2.

Connell, Raewyn. 2015. 'Meeting at the Edge of Fear: Theory on a World Scale'. *Feminist Theory* 16 (1): 49–66.

Connell, Raewyn. 2018. 'Decolonizing Sociology'. *Contemporary Sociology* 47 (4): 399–407.

Connell, Raewyn. 2019. *The Good University: What Universities Actually Do and Why It's Time for Radical Change*. London: Zed Books.

Connell, Raewyn, Fran Collyer, João Maia and Robert Morrell. 2017. 'Toward a Global Sociology of Knowledge:

Post-Colonial Realities and Intellectual Practices'. *International Sociology* 32 (1): 21–37.

Connell, Raewyn, Rebecca Pearse, Fran Collyer, João Marcelo Maia and Robert Morrell. 2018. 'Negotiating with the North: How Southern-Tier Intellectual Workers Deal with the Global Economy of Knowledge'. *The Sociological Review* 66 (1): 41–57.

Cooper, Anna Julia. 1990 [1892]. *A Voice from the South.* Oxford: Oxford University Press.

Cordeiro, Veridiana Domingos, and Hugo Neri. 2019. *Sociology in Brazil: A Brief Institutional and Intellectual History.* London: Palgrave.

Costa, Sérgio. 2007. '"Deprovincializing" Sociology: The Post Colonial Contribution'. *Revista Brasileira de Ciências Sociais* 3: 1–20.

Cox, Oliver C. 1959. *Caste, Class, and Race: A Study in Social Dynamics.* New York, NY: Monthly Review Press.

Crenshaw, Kimberle. 1989. 'Demarginalizing the Intersection of Race and Sex: A Black Feminist Critique of Antidiscrimination Doctrine, Feminist Theory and Antiracist Politics'. *University of Chicago Legal Forum* 1: 139–67.

Crothers, Charles. 2018. *Sociologies of New Zealand.* London: Palgrave.

Davis, Angela. 1983. *Women, Race & Class.* New York, NY: Vintage.

Demuro, Eugenia. 2015. 'Embers of the Past: The Coloniality of Time'. *Postcolonial Studies* 18 (1): 88–91.

Denzin, Norman K. 1997. *Interpretive Ethnography: Ethnographic Practices for the 21st Century.* Thousand Oaks, CA: SAGE.

Denzin, Norman K. 2017. 'Critical Qualitative Inquiry'. *Qualitative Inquiry* 23 (1): 8–16.

Denzin, Norman K., Yvonna S. Lincoln and Linda Tuhiwai Smith. 2008. *Handbook of Critical and Indigenous Methodologies.* London: SAGE.

Dietz, Thomas, Rachael L. Shwom and Cameron T. Whitley. 2020. 'Climate Change and Society'. *Annual Review of Sociology* 46 (1).

Domingues, José Maurício. 2009. 'Global Modernization, "Coloniality" and a Critical Sociology for Contemporary Latin America'. *Theory, Culture & Society* 26 (1): 112–33.

Du Bois, W. E. Burghardt. 1898. 'The Study of the Negro Problems'. *The Annals of the American Academy of Political and Social Science* 11: 1–23.

Du Bois, W. E. Burghardt. 1954. 'The Status of Colonialism'. Special Collections and University Archives, University of Massachusetts Amherst Libraries. https://credo.library.umass.edu/view/full/mums312-b204-i042.

Du Bois, W. E. Burghardt. 1967 [1899]. *The Philadelphia Negro: A Social Study*. New York, NY: Schocken Books.

Du Bois, W. E. Burghardt. 1968. *The Autobiography of W.E.B. Du Bois: A Soliloquy on Viewing My Life from the Final Decade of Its First Century*. Edited by Herbert Aptheker. New York, NY: International.

Du Bois, W. E. Burghardt. 2007 [1896]. *Black Folk: Then and Now*. Oxford: Oxford University Press.

Du Bois, W. E. Burghardt. 2007 [1903]. *The Souls of Black Folk*. Oxford: Oxford University Press.

Du Bois, W. E. Burghardt. 2007 [1940]. *Dusk of Dawn: An Essay Toward an Autobiography of a Race Concept*. Oxford: Oxford University Press.

Du Bois, W. E. Burghardt. 2007 [1947]. *The World and Africa: An Inquiry into the Part which Africa Has Played in World History and Color and Democracy*. Oxford: Oxford University Press.

Du Bois, W. E. Burghardt. 2008 [1920]. 'The Souls of White Folk'. In *Classical and Contemporary Sociological Theory: Text and Readings*, edited by Scott Appelrouth and Laura Desfor Edles, 305–9. Los Angeles, CA: Pine Forge Press.

Du Bois, W. E. Burghardt. 2012 [1920]. *Darkwater: Voices from Within the Veil*. North Chelmsford, MA: Courier.

Du Bois, W. E. Burghardt. 2014 [1935]. *Black Reconstruction in America: An Essay Toward a History of the Part which Black Folk Played in the Attempt to Reconstruct Democracy in America, 1860–1880*. Oxford: Oxford University Press.

Dubois, Laurent. 2004. *Avengers of the New World: The*

Story of the Haitian Revolution. Cambridge, MA: Harvard University Press.

Dubois, Laurent. 2012. *Haiti: The Aftershocks of History*. New York, NY: Henry Holt.

Dufoix, Stéphane. 2018. 'Coming to Terms with Western Social Science: Three Historical Lessons from Asia'. *Journal of Glocal Studies* 5: 49–71.

Durkheim, Émile. 1997 [1893]. *The Division of Labor in Society*. New York, NY: Simon & Schuster.

Durkheim, Émile. 2008 [1912]. *The Elementary Forms of the Religious Life*. North Chelmsford, MA: Courier.

Durkheim, Émile. 2010 [1953]. *Sociology and Philosophy*. Translated by D. F. Pocock. Abingdon: Routledge.

Durkheim, Émile. 2014 [1938]. *The Rules of Sociological Method: And Selected Texts on Sociology and Its Method*. New York, NY: Simon & Schuster.

Dussel, Enrique D. 1999. 'Beyond Eurocentrism: The World-System and the Limits of Modernity'. In *The Cultures of Globalization*, edited by Fredric Jameson and Masao Miyoshi, 3–31. Durham, NC: Duke University Press.

Dussel, Enrique D. 2002. 'World-System and "Trans"-Modernity'. Translated by Alessandro Fornazzari. *Nepantla: Views from South* 3 (2): 221–44.

Elias, Norbert. 1982 [1939]. *The Civilizing Process*. Oxford: Blackwell.

Escobar, Arturo. 2007. 'Worlds and Knowledges Otherwise'. *Cultural Studies* 21 (2–3): 179–210.

Fanon, Frantz. 1963 [1961]. *The Wretched of the Earth*. New York, NY: Grove Weidenfeld.

Fanon, Frantz. 2008 [1952]. *Black Skin, White Masks*. London: Pluto.

Fields, Karen E. 2002. 'Individuality and the Intellectuals: An Imaginary Conversation between W. E. B. Du Bois and Emile Durkheim'. *Theory and Society* 31 (4): 435–62.

Figueroa Helland, Leonardo E., and Tim Lindgren. 2016. 'What Goes Around Comes Around: From the Coloniality of Power to the Crisis of Civilization'. *Journal of World-Systems Research* 22 (2): 430–62.

Fitzhugh George. 1854. *Sociology for the South, or the Failure of Free Society*. Richmond, VA: A. Morris.

Foucault, Michel. 1990 [1976]. *The History of Sexuality: An Introduction: Vol. 1*. New York, NY: Vintage.

Foucault, Michel. 1991 [1979]. 'Between "Words" and "Things" During May '68'. In *Remarks on Marx: Conversations with Duccio Trombador*, 131–46. New York, NY: Semiotext(e).

Foucault, Michel. 2010 [1978]. 'What Are the Iranians Dreaming About?' In *Foucault and the Iranian Revolution: Gender and the Seductions of Islamism*, edited by Janet Afary and Kevin B. Anderson, 203–9. Chicago, IL: University of Chicago Press.

Foucault, Michel. 2012 [1984]. *The History of Sexuality: The Use of Pleasure: Vol. 2*. New York, NY: Vintage.

Foucault, Michel. 2012 [1988]. *The History of Sexuality: The Care of the Self: Vol. 3*. New York, NY: Vintage.

Foucault, Michel. 2019 [1975]. *Discipline and Punish: The Birth of the Prison*. London: Penguin.

Frazier, E. Franklin. 1947. 'Sociological Theory and Race Relations'. *American Sociological Review* 12 (3): 265.

Friedman, Julian R. 1951. Review of *Principles and Methods of Colonial Administration*. *The British Journal of Sociology* 2 (4): 377.

Fryer, Peter. 1984. *Staying Power: The History of Black People in Britain*. London: Pluto.

Galton, Francis. 1904. 'Eugenics: Its Definition, Scope, and Aims'. *American Journal of Sociology* 10 (1): 1–25.

Gamage, Siri. 2018. 'Indigenous and Postcolonial Sociology in South Asia: Challenges and Possibilities'. *Sri Lanka Journal of Social Sciences* 41 (2): 83–99.

Gareau, Frederick H. 1988. 'Another Type of Third World Dependency: The Social Sciences'. *International Sociology* 3 (2): 171–8.

Getachew, Adom. 2016. 'Universalism After the Post-Colonial Turn: Interpreting the Haitian Revolution'. *Political Theory* 44 (6): 821–45.

Giddens, Anthony. 1984. *The Constitution of Society: Outline of the Theory of Structuration*. Cambridge: Polity.

Giddens, Anthony. 1990. *The Consequences of Modernity.* Stanford, CA: Stanford University Press.

Giddens, Anthony. 2002. *Runaway World: How Globalisation Is Reshaping Our Lives.* 2nd edn. London: Profile Books.

Giddings, Franklin H. 1898. 'Imperialism?' *Political Science Quarterly* 13 (4): 585–605.

Giddings, Franklin H. 1901. *Democracy and Empire: With Studies of Their Psychological, Economic, and Moral Foundations.* London: Macmillan.

Giddings, Franklin H. 1911. 'The Relation of Social Theory to Public Policy'. *American Journal of Sociology* 16 (5): 577–92.

Gilroy, Paul. 1993. *The Black Atlantic: Modernity and Double Consciousness.* Cambridge, MA: Harvard University Press.

Gilroy, Paul. 2004. *After Empire: Melancholia or Convivial Culture?* London: Routledge.

Glenn, Evelyn Nakano. 2015. 'Settler Colonialism as Structure: A Framework for Comparative Studies of U.S. Race and Gender Formation'. *Sociology of Race and Ethnicity* 1 (1): 52–72.

Go, Julian. 2008. 'Global Fields and Imperial Forms: Field Theory and the British and American Empires'. *Sociological Theory* 26 (3): 201–29.

Go, Julian. 2009. 'The "New" Sociology of Empire and Colonialism'. *Sociology Compass* 3 (5): 775–88.

Go, Julian. 2011. *Patterns of Empire: The British and American Empires, 1688 to the Present.* Cambridge: Cambridge University Press.

Go, Julian. 2013a. 'The Emergence of American Sociology in the Context of Empire'. In *Sociology & Empire: The Imperial Entanglements of a Discipline*, edited by George Steinmetz, 83–103. Durham, NC: Duke University Press.

Go, Julian. 2013b. 'Decolonizing Bourdieu: Colonial and Postcolonial Theory in Pierre Bourdieu's Early Work'. *Sociological Theory* 31 (1): 49–74.

Go, Julian. 2014. 'Beyond Metrocentrism: From Empire to Globalism in Early US Sociology'. *Journal of Classical Sociology* 14 (2): 178–202.

Go, Julian. 2016a. *Postcolonial Thought and Social Theory.* New York, NY: Oxford University Press.

Go, Julian. 2016b. 'Globalizing Sociology, Turning South: Perspectival Realism and the Southern Standpoint'. *Sociologica* 2: 1–42.

Go, Julian. 2018. 'Postcolonial Possibilities for the Sociology of Race'. *Sociology of Race and Ethnicity* 4 (4): 439–51.

Goody, Jack. 2003. 'The "Civilizing Process" in Ghana'. *European Journal of Sociology/Archives Européennes de Sociologie* 44 (1): 61–73.

Gopal, Priyamvada. 2019. *Insurgent Empire: Anticolonialism and the Making of British Dissent.* London: Verso.

Gordon, Lewis. 2007. 'Through the Hellish Zone of Nonbeing: Thinking through Fanon, Disaster, and the Damned of the Earth'. *Human Architecture: Journal of the Sociology of Self- Knowledge* 5 (3): 5–12.

Goswami, Namita. 2013. 'The (M)Other of All Posts: Postcolonial Melancholia in the Age of Global Warming'. *Critical Philosophy of Race* 1 (1): 104–20.

Grant, Harriet. 2019. '"Prejudiced" Home Office Refusing Visas to African Researchers'. *The Observer*, 8 June, sec. Politics. https://www.theguardian.com/politics/2019/jun/08/home-office-racist-refusing-research-visas-africans.

Grosfoguel, Ramón. 2007. 'The Epistemic Decolonial Turn: Beyond Political-Economy Paradigms'. *Cultural Studies* 21 (2–3): 211–23.

Grosfoguel, Ramón. 2017. 'Decolonizing Western Universalisms: Decolonial Pluri-Versalism from Aimé Césaire to the Zapatistas'. In *Towards a Just Curriculum Theory: The Epistemicide*, edited by João M. Paraskeva, 147–64. New York, NY: Routledge.

Gumplowicz, Ludwig. 1883. *Der Rassenkampf.* Innsbruck: Universitäts-Verlag Wagner.

Gutting, Gary. 2005. *Foucault: A Very Short Introduction.* Oxford: Oxford University Press.

Habermas, Jürgen. 1976. *Legitimation Crisis.* Translated by Thomas McCarthy. London: Heinemann.

Habermas, Jürgen. 2015 [1962]. *The Structural Transformation of the Public Sphere: An Inquiry into a*

Category of Bourgeois Society. Hoboken, NJ: John Wiley & Sons.

Hall, Stuart. 1991. 'Old and New Identities, Old and New Ethnicities'. In *Culture, Globalization and the World System: Contemporary Conditions for the Representation of Identity*, edited by Anthony King, 41–68. Minneapolis, MN: University of Minnesota Press.

Hall, Stuart. 1992. 'The West and the Rest'. In *Formations of Modernity*, edited by Stuart Hall and Bram Gieben, 275–332. Cambridge: Polity.

Hall, Stuart. 1996. 'When Was "the Post-Colonial"? Thinking at the Limit'. In *The Post-Colonial Question: Common Skies, Divided Horizons*, edited by Iain Chambers and Lidia Curti, 242–60. London: Routledge.

Hammer, Ricarda, and Alexandre I. R. White. 2018. 'Toward a Sociology of Colonial Subjectivity: Political Agency in Haiti and Liberia'. *Sociology of Race and Ethnicity*, September.

Hanafi, Sari. 2010. 'Palestinian Sociological Production: Funding and National Considerations'. In *The ISA Handbook of Diverse Sociological Traditions*, edited by Sujata Patel, 257–67. Los Angeles, CA: SAGE.

Harding, Sandra. 1987. *Feminism and Methodology: Social Science Issues*. Bloomington, IN: Indiana University Press.

Harding, Sandra. 1991. *Whose Science? Whose Knowledge? Thinking from Women's Lives*. Ithaca, NY: Cornell University Press.

Harding, Sandra. 2004. *The Feminist Standpoint Theory Reader: Intellectual and Political Controversies*. London: Routledge.

Harley, Kirsten, and Gary Wickham. 2014. *Australian Sociology: Fragility, Survival, Rivalry*. London: Palgrave.

Henriques, Fernando. 1951. 'Colour Values in Jamaican Society'. *The British Journal of Sociology* 2 (2): 115–21.

Holmwood, John, and John Scott. 2014. *The Palgrave Handbook of Sociology in Britain*. London: Palgrave.

Horkheimer, Max, and Theodor W. Adorno. 2002 [1944]. *Dialectic of Enlightenment: Philosophical Fragments*.

Edited by Gunzelin Schmid Noerr. Stanford, CA: Stanford University Press.

Hountondji, Paulin. 1997. *Endogenous Knowledge: Research Trails*. Dakar: CODESRIA.

Hughey, Matthew W., and Devon R. Goss. 2018. '"With Whom No White Scholar Can Compare": Academic Interpretations of the Relationship between W.E.B. Du Bois and Max Weber'. *The American Sociologist* 49 (2): 181–217.

Huizer, Gerrit, and Bruce Mannheim. 1979. *The Politics of Anthropology: From Colonialism and Sexism Toward a View from Below*. The Hague: Mouton.

Hund, Wulf D. 2015. 'Racist King Kong Fantasies. From Shakespeare's Monster to Stalin's Ape-Man'. In *Simianization: Apes, Gender, Class, and Race*, edited by Wulf D. Hund, Charles W. Mills and Silvia Sebastiani, 43–73. Berlin: Lit Verlag.

Huntington, Ellsworth. 1914. 'The Adaptability of the White Man to Tropical America'. *The Journal of Race Development* 5 (2): 185–211.

Ince, Onur Ulas. 2012. 'Not a Partnership in Pepper, Coffee, Calico, or Tobacco: Edmund Burke and the Vicissitudes of Colonial Capitalism'. *Polity* 44 (3): 340–72.

Itzigsohn, José, and Karida L. Brown. 2020. *The Sociology of W. E. B. Du Bois: Racialized Modernity and the Global Color Line*. New York, NY: NYU Press.

James, C. L. R. 2001 [1938]. *The Black Jacobins: Toussaint L'Ouverture and the San Domingo Revolution*. London: Penguin.

Jenkins, Richard. 2014. *Pierre Bourdieu*. London: Routledge.

Kauanui, J. Kēhaulani. 2016. '"A Structure, Not an Event": Settler Colonialism and Enduring Indigeneity'. *Lateral: Journal of the Cultural Studies Association* 5 (1).

Keating, AnaLouise. 2009. 'Introduction: Reading Gloria Anzaldúa, Reading Ourselves … Complex Intimacies, Intricate Connections'. In *The Gloria Anzladúa Reader*, edited by AnaLouise Keating, 1–15. Durham, NC: Duke University Press.

Keller, Albert G. 1906. 'The Value of the Study of Colonies

for Sociology'. *American Journal of Sociology* 12 (3): 417–20.

Kenyatta, Jomo. 1979 [1938]. *Facing Mount Kenya*. London: Heinemann.

Khaldūn, Ibn. 2015 [1370]. *The Muqaddimah: An Introduction to History – Abridged Edition*. Princeton, NJ: Princeton University Press.

Koch, Alexander, Chris Brierley, Mark M. Maslin and Simon L. Lewis. 2019. 'Earth System Impacts of the European Arrival and Great Dying in the Americas after 1492'. *Quaternary Science Reviews* 207 (March): 13–36.

Kovach, Margaret. 2010. *Indigenous Methodologies: Characteristics, Conversations, and Contexts*. Toronto: University of Toronto Press.

Kuehn, Julia. 2011. 'Exotic Harem Paintings: Gender, Documentation, and Imagination'. *Frontiers: A Journal of Women Studies* 32 (2): 31–63.

Kuper, Leo. 1953. 'The Background to Passive Resistance (South Africa, 1952)'. *The British Journal of Sociology* 4 (3): 243–56.

Kurasawa, Fuyuki. 2013. 'The Durkheimian School and Colonialism: Exploring the Constitutive Paradox'. In *Sociology & Empire: The Imperial Entanglements of a Discipline*, edited by George Steinmetz, 188–209. Durham, NC: Duke University Press.

Lamble, Lucy. 2013. 'Cashew Nut Workers Suffer "Appalling" Conditions as Global Slump Dents Profits'. *The Guardian*, 2 November. https://www. theguardian.com/global-development/2013/nov/02/ cashew-nut-workers-pay-conditions-profits.

Lamont, Michèle. 2009. *How Professors Think*. Cambridge, MA: Harvard University Press.

Lamont, Michèle. 2012. 'How Has Bourdieu Been Good to Think With? The Case of the United States'. *Sociological Forum* 27 (1): 228–37.

Lane, Linda, and Hauwa Mahdi. 2013. 'Fanon Revisited: Race, Gender and Coloniality Vis-à-Vis Skin Colour'. In *The Melanin Millennium: Skin Color as 21st Century*

International Discourse, edited by Ronald E. Hall, 169–81. Dordrecht: Springer.

Leach, E. R. 1953. Review of *Survey of African Marriage and Family Life*, by Arthur Phillips, L. P. Mair and Lyndon Harries. *The British Journal of Sociology* 4 (3): 286–8.

Lee, Namhee. 2007. *The Making of Minjung: Democracy and the Politics of Representation in South Korea*. Ithaca, NY: Cornell University Press.

Leonardo, Zeus. 2002. 'The Souls of White Folk: Critical Pedagogy, Whiteness Studies, and Globalization Discourse'. *Race, Ethnicity and Education* 5 (1): 29–50.

Lewis, Laura A. 2012. *Chocolate and Corn Flour: History, Race, and Place in the Making of 'Black' Mexico*. Durham, NC: Duke University Press.

Lipsitz, George. 1998. *The Possessive Investment in Whiteness: How White People Profit from Identity Politics*. Philadelphia, PA: Temple University Press.

Loveman, Mara. 2009a. 'The Race to Progress: Census Taking and Nation Making in Brazil (1870–1920)'. *Hispanic American Historical Review* 89 (3): 435–70.

Loveman, Mara. 2009b. 'Whiteness in Latin America: Measurement and Meaning in National Censuses (1850–1950)'. *Journal de La Société des Américanistes* 95 (2): 207–34.

Loveman, Mara. 2014. *National Colors: Racial Classification and the State in Latin America*. Oxford: Oxford University Press.

Loveman, Mara, Jeronimo O. Muniz and Stanley R. Bailey. 2012. 'Brazil in Black and White? Race Categories, the Census, and the Study of Inequality'. *Ethnic and Racial Studies* 35 (8): 1466–83.

Lugones, María. 2007. 'Heterosexualism and the Colonial/Modern Gender System'. *Hypatia* 22 (1): 186–209.

Lugones, María. 2010. 'Toward a Decolonial Feminism'. *Hypatia* 25 (4): 742–59.

Lugones, María. 2016. 'The Coloniality of Gender'. In *The Palgrave Handbook of Gender and Development*, edited by Wendy Harcourt, 13–33. London: Palgrave Macmillan.

Lusane, Clarence. 2004. *Hitler's Black Victims: The*

Historical Experiences of European Blacks, Africans and African Americans During the Nazi Era. New York, NY: Routledge.

Magubane, Bernard Makhosezwe. 2000. 'Imperialism and the Making of the South African Working Class'. In *African Sociology – Towards a Critical Perspective: The Collected Essays of Bernard Makhosezwe Magubane*, 335–76. Trenton, NJ: Africa World Press.

Magubane, Zine. 2013. 'Common Skies and Divided Horizons? Sociology, Race, and Postcolonial Studies'. *Political Power and Social Theory* 24: 81–116.

Magubane, Zine. 2016. 'American Sociology's Racial Ontology: Remembering Slavery, Deconstructing Modernity, and Charting the Future of Global Historical Sociology'. *Cultural Sociology* 10 (3): 369–84.

Maia, Joao Marcelo. 2014. 'History of Sociology and the Quest for Intellectual Autonomy in the Global South: The Cases of Alberto Guerreiro Ramos and Syed Hussein Alatas'. *Current Sociology* 62 (7): 1097–115.

Maldonado-Torres, Nelson. 2007. 'On the Coloniality of Being'. *Cultural Studies* 21 (2–3): 240–70.

Maldonado-Torres, Nelson. 2017. 'Against Coloniality: On the Meaning and Significance of the Decolonial Turn'. In *Towards a Just Curriculum Theory: The Epistemicide*, edited by João M. Paraskeva, 165–80. New York, NY: Routledge.

Mandle, Jay. 1967. 'Neo-Imperialism: An Essay in Definition Comment'. *Social and Economic Studies* 16 (3): 318–25.

Mann, Michael. 2012a. *The Sources of Social Power: Vol. 1, A History of Power from the Beginning to AD 1760*. Cambridge: Cambridge University Press.

Mann, Michael. 2012b. *The Sources of Social Power: Vol. 2, The Rise of Classes and Nation-States, 1760–1914*. Cambridge: Cambridge University Press.

Mann, Michael. 2012c. *The Sources of Social Power: Vol. 3, Global Empires and Revolution, 1890–1945*. Cambridge: Cambridge University Press.

Mann, Michael. 2012d. *The Sources of Social Power: Vol.*

4, *Globalizations, 1945–2011*. Cambridge: Cambridge University Press.

Marx, Karl. 1853. 'The British Rule in India'. *New-York Daily Tribune*, 25 June.

Marx, Karl. 1973 [1939]. *Grundrisse: Foundations of the Critique of Political Economy*. London: Penguin.

Marx, Karl. 1988. *Marx and the French Revolution*. Chicago, IL: University of Chicago Press.

Marx, Karl. 1998 [1894]. *Capital: Vol. 3*. London: Lawrence & Wishart.

Marx, Karl. 2004 [1867]. *Capital: A Critique of Political Economy*. London: Penguin.

Marx, Karl. 2007 [1932]. *Economic and Philosophic Manuscripts of 1844*. North Chelmsford, MA: Courier.

Mbembe, Achille. 2016. 'Decolonizing the University: New Directions'. *Arts and Humanities in Higher Education* 15 (1): 29–45.

McNay, Lois. 2013. *Foucault: A Critical Introduction*. Hoboken, NJ: John Wiley & Sons.

Medien, Kathryn. 2019. 'Foucault in Tunisia: The Encounter with Intolerable Power'. *The Sociological Review* 68 (3): 492–507.

Meer, Nasar. 2018. '"Race" and "Post-Colonialism": Should One Come Before the Other?' *Ethnic and Racial Studies* 41 (6): 1163–81.

Meghji, Ali. 2017a. 'The Enduring Legacy of Stuart Hall: Politics Then and Now'. *Cultural Studies* 31 (6): 970–3.

Meghji, Ali. 2017b. 'A Relational Study of the Black Middle Classes and Globalised White Hegemony: Identities, Interactions, and Ideologies in the United States, United Kingdom, and South Africa'. *Sociology Compass* 11 (9).

Meghji, Ali. 2019a. 'White Power, Racialized Regimes of Truth, and (In)Validity'. *Sentio* 1 (1): 36–41.

Meghji, Ali. 2019b. *Black Middle Class Britannia*. Manchester: Manchester University Press.

Meller, Helen. 2005. *Patrick Geddes: Social Evolutionist and City Planner*. London: Routledge.

Meyer, Manulani Aluli. 2008. 'Indigenous and Authentic:

Hawaiian Epistemology and the Triangulation of Meaning'. In *Handbook of Critical and Indigenous Methodologies*, edited by Norman Denzin, Yvonna Lincoln and Linda Smith, 217–32. Thousand Oaks, CA: SAGE.

Mignolo, Walter. 2002. 'The Geopolitics of Knowledge and the Colonial Difference'. *The South Atlantic Quarterly* 101 (1): 57–96.

Mignolo, Walter. 2007. 'Delinking: The Rhetoric of Modernity, the Logic of Coloniality and the Grammar of De-Coloniality'. *Cultural Studies* 21 (2–3): 449–514.

Mignolo, Walter. 2011a. 'Epistemic Disobedience and the Decolonial Option: A Manifesto'. *TRANSMODERNITY: Journal of Peripheral Cultural Production of the Luso-Hispanic World* 1 (2): 44–66.

Mignolo, Walter. 2011b. *The Darker Side of Western Modernity: Global Futures, Decolonial Options*. Durham, NC: Duke University Press.

Mignolo, Walter. 2012. 'Coloniality at Large: Time and the Colonial Difference'. In *Enchantments of Modernity: Empire, Nation, Globalization*, edited by Saurabh Dube, 62–95. London: Routledge.

Mignolo, Walter, and Catherine Walsh. 2018. *On Decoloniality: Concepts, Analytics, Praxis*. Durham, NC: Duke University Press.

Mills, Charles W. 1997. *The Racial Contract*. Ithaca, NY: Cornell University Press.

Mills, Charles W. 2014. 'White Time: The Chronic Injustice of Ideal Theory'. *Du Bois Review: Social Science Research on Race* 11 (1): 27–42.

Mills, Sara. 2003. *Michel Foucault*. London: Routledge.

Morris, Aldon. 2017. *The Scholar Denied: W. E. B. Du Bois and the Birth of Modern Sociology*. Oakland, CA: University of California Press.

Morrison, Ken. 1995. *Marx, Durkheim, Weber: Formations of Modern Social Thought*. London: SAGE.

Myoung-Kyu, Park, and Chang Kyung-Sup. 1999. 'Sociology Between Western Theory and Korean Reality: Accommodation, Tension and a Search for Alternatives'. *International Sociology* 14 (2): 139–56.

Olutayo, Akinpelu Olanrewaju. 2014. '"Verstehen", Everyday Sociology and Development: Incorporating African Indigenous Knowledge'. *Critical Sociology* 40 (2): 229–38.

Omi, Michael, and Howard Winant. 1994. *Racial Formation in the United States: From the 1960s to the 1990s*. New York, NY: Routledge.

Omobowale, Ayokunle Olumuyiwa, and Olayinka Akanle. 2017. '*Asuwada* Epistemology and Globalised Sociology: Challenges of the South'. *Sociology* 51 (1): 43–59.

Onwuzuruigbo, Ifeanyi. 2018. 'Indigenising Eurocentric Sociology: The "Captive Mind" and Five Decades of Sociology in Nigeria'. *Current Sociology* 66 (6): 831–48.

Outhwaite, William. 2009. 'Canon Formation in Late 20th-Century British Sociology'. *Sociology* 43 (6): 1029–45.

Oyěwùmí, Oyèrónkẹ́. 1997. *The Invention of Women: Making an African Sense of Western Gender Discourses*. Minneapolis, MN: University of Minnesota Press.

Palacios, Marco. 2002. *Coffee in Colombia, 1850–1970: An Economic, Social and Political History*. Cambridge: Cambridge University Press.

Park, Robert. 1906. 'Tuskegee and Its Mission'. *The Colored American Magazine* 14: 347–54.

Park, Robert. 1912. 'Education by Cultural Groups'. *The Southern Workman* 41: 369–77.

Patel, Sujata. 2010. 'At Crossroads: Sociology in India'. In *The ISA Handbook of Diverse Sociological Traditions*, edited by Sujata Patel, 280–91. Los Angeles, CA: SAGE.

Patel, Sujata. 2014. 'Afterword: Doing Global Sociology: Issues, Problems and Challenges'. *Current Sociology* 62 (4): 603–13.

Patel, Sujata. 2016. 'The Profession and Its Association: Five Decades of the Indian Sociological Society'. *International Sociology* 17 (2): 269–84.

Patel, Sujata. 2017. 'Colonial Modernity and Methodological Nationalism: The Structuring of Sociological Traditions of India'. *Sociological Bulletin* 66 (2): 125–44.

Patnaik, Utsa. 2017. 'Revisiting the "Drain", or Transfer

from India to Britain in the Context of Global Diffusion of Capitalism'. In *Agrarian and Other Histories: Essays for Binay Bhushan Chaudhuri*, edited by Shubhra Chakrabarti and Utsa Patnaik, 278–317. New Delhi: Tulika Books.

Pereyra, Diego Ezequiel. 2010. 'Dilemmas, Challenges and Uncertain Boundaries of Argentinian Sociology'. In *The ISA Handbook of Diverse Sociological Traditions*, edited by Sujata Patel, 212–22. Los Angeles, CA: SAGE.

Pinto, Céli Regina Jardim. 2014. 'O feminismo bem-comportado de Heleieth Saffioti (presença do marxismo)'. *Revista Estudos Feministas* 22 (1): 321–33.

Puwar, Nirmal. 2009. 'Sensing a Post-Colonial Bourdieu: An Introduction'. *The Sociological Review* 57 (3): 371–84.

Puwar, Nirmal. 2019. 'Puzzlement of a Déjà Vu: Illuminaries of the Global South'. *The Sociological Review*, Online First, 1–17.

Quijano, Aníbal. 2007. 'Coloniality and Modernity/Rationality'. *Cultural Studies* 21 (2–3): 168–78.

Quijano, Aníbal, and Immanuel Wallerstein. 1992. 'Americanity as a Concept; or, The Americas in the Modern World-System'. *International Social Science Journal* 44 (4): 549–57.

Rabaka, Reiland. 2009. *Africana Critical Theory: Reconstructing the Black Radical Tradition, from W. E. B. Du Bois and C. L. R. James to Frantz Fanon and Amilcar Cabral*. Lanham, MD: Lexington Books.

Ram, Uri. 2018. *Israeli Sociology: Text in Context*. London: Palgrave.

Reed, Isaac Ariail. 2013. 'Theoretical Labors Necessary for a Global Sociology: Critique of Raewyn Connell's Southern Theory'. *Decentering Social Theory*, special issue of *Political Power and Social Theory* 25: 151–71.

Rizal, José. 2019 [1890]. *The Indolence of the Filipino*. Glasgow: Good Press.

Roberts, Celia, and Raewyn Connell. 2016. 'Feminist Theory and the Global South'. *Feminist Theory* 17 (2): 135–40.

Rodney, Walter. 2018 [1972]. *How Europe Underdeveloped Africa*. London: Verso.

Roediger, David. 2017. *Class, Race, and Marxism*. London: Verso.

Ross, Edward A. 1901. 'The Causes of Race Superiority'. *The Annals of the American Academy of Political and Social Science* 18: 67–89.

Saffari, Siavash. 2015. 'Rethinking the Islam/Modernity Binary: Ali Shariati and Religiously Mediated Discourse of Sociopolitical Development'. *Middle East Critique* 24 (3): 231–50.

Saïd, Edward. 1979. *Orientalism*. London: Penguin.

Saïd, Edward. 1989. 'Representing the Colonized: Anthropology's Interlocutors'. *Critical Inquiry* 15: 205–25.

Saïd, Edward. 1994. *Culture and Imperialism*. London: Random House.

Saldívar, Emiko, and Casey Walsh. 2014. 'Racial and Ethnic Identities in Mexican Statistics'. *Journal of Iberian and Latin American Research* 20 (3): 455–75.

Salem, Sara. 2020. *Anticolonial Afterlives in Egypt: The Politics of Hegemony*. Cambridge: Cambridge University Press.

Sall, Dialika, and Shamus Khan. 2017. 'What Elite Theory Should Have Learned, and Can Still Learn, from W.E.B. DuBois'. *Ethnic and Racial Studies* 40 (3): 512–14.

Sall, Ebrima, and Jean-Bernard Ouedraogo. 2010. 'Sociology in West Africa: Challenges and Obstacles to Academic Autonomy'. In *The ISA Handbook of Diverse Sociological Traditions*, edited by Sujata Patel, 225–34. Los Angeles, CA: SAGE.

Sanderson, Henry. 2019. 'Congo, Child Labour and Your Electric Car'. *The Financial Times*, 6 July. https://www.ft.com/content/c6909812-9ce4-11e9-9c06-a4640c9feebb.

Santos, Boaventura de Sousa. 2014. *Epistemologies of the South: Justice Against Epistemicide*. New York, NY: Routledge.

Sarkar, Benoy Kumar. 1912. *The Science of History and the Hope of Mankind*. Miami, FL: HardPress.

Scaff, Lawrence A. 1998. 'The "Cool Objectivity of

Sociation": Max Weber and Marianne Weber in America'. *History of the Human Sciences* 11 (2): 61–82.

Scott, John. 2010. 'Diversity, Dominance, and Plurality in British Sociology'. In *The ISA Handbook of Diverse Sociological Traditions*, edited by Sujata Patel, 94–104. Los Angeles, CA: SAGE.

Sealey-Huggins, Leon. 2017. '"1.5°C to Stay Alive": Climate Change, Imperialism and Justice for the Caribbean'. *Third World Quarterly* 38 (11): 2444–63.

Sealey-Huggins, Leon. 2018. '"The Climate Crisis Is a Racist Crisis": Structural Racism, Inequality and Climate Change'. In *The Fire Now: Anti-Racist Scholarship in Times of Explicit Racial Violence*, edited by Azeezat Johnson, Remi Joseph-Salisbury and Beth Kamunge, 149–68. London: Zed Books.

Shari'ati, Ali. 1980. *Marxism and Other Western Fallacies: An Islamic Critique*. Markfield: Islamic Foundation Press.

Shari'ati, Ali. 1986. *What Is to Be Done: The Enlightened Thinkers and an Islamic Renaissance*. Edited by Farhang Rajaee. Houston, TX: Institute for Research and Islamic Studies.

Simons, Sarah E. 1901. 'Social Assimilation. VII: Assimilation in the Modern World'. *American Journal of Sociology* 7 (2): 234–48.

Slabodsky, Santiago. 2009. 'De-Colonial Jewish Thought and the Americas'. In *Postcolonial Philosophy of Religion*, edited by Purushottama Bilimoria and Andrew B. Irvine, 251–72. New York, NY: Springer.

Slabodsky, Santiago. 2010. 'Emmanuel Levinas's Geopolitics: Overlooked Conversations Between Rabbinical and Third World Decolonialisms'. *The Journal of Jewish Thought and Philosophy* 18 (2): 147–65.

Slabodsky, Santiago. 2016. 'In Network: The Case for Decolonial Jewish Thought'. *Politics and Religion Journal* 10 (2): 151–71.

Small, Albion W. 1906. 'The Relation Between Sociology and Other Sciences'. *American Journal of Sociology* 12 (1): 11–31.

Smith, Linda Tuhiwai. 2008 [1999]. *Decolonizing*

Methodologies: Research and Indigeneous Peoples. London: Zed Books.

Sofer, Cyril, and Rhona Ross. 1951. 'Some Characteristics of an East African European Population'. *The British Journal of Sociology* 2 (4): 315–27.

Solomos, John. 2014. 'Stuart Hall: Articulations of Race, Class and Identity'. *Ethnic and Racial Studies* 37 (10): 1667–75.

Spencer, Herbert. 2010 [1895]. *The Principles of Sociology: Vol. 2.* Kootenay Bay, BC: Timeless Books.

Spivak, Gayatri Chakravorty. 2010 [1985]. 'Can the Subaltern Speak?' In *Can the Subaltern Speak?: Reflections on the History of an Idea*, edited by Rosalind Morris, 21–80. New York, NY: Columbia University Press.

Steinmetz, George. 2008. 'The Colonial State as a Social Field: Ethnographic Capital and Native Policy in the German Overseas Empire before 1914'. *American Sociological Review* 73 (4): 589–612.

Steinmetz, George. 2009. 'Neo-Bourdieusian Theory and the Question of Scientific Autonomy: German Sociologists and Empire, 1890s–1940s'. *Political Power and Social Theory* 20: 71–131.

Steinmetz, George. 2013. 'A Child of the Empire: British Sociology and Colonialism, 1940s–1960s'. *Journal of the History of the Behavioral Sciences* 49 (4): 353–78.

Steinmetz, George. 2014. 'The Sociology of Empires, Colonies, and Postcolonialism'. *Annual Review of Sociology* 40 (1): 77–103.

Steinmetz, George. 2017. 'Sociology and Colonialism in the British and French Empires, 1945–1965'. *The Journal of Modern History* 89 (3): 601–48.

Stewart-Harawira, M. 2005. *The New Imperial Order: Indigenous Responses to Globalization.* London: Zed Books.

Swartz, David. 1997. *Culture & Power: The Sociology of Pierre Bourdieu.* Chicago, IL: University of Chicago Press.

Thiong'o, Ngũgĩ wa. 1987. *Decolonising the Mind: The Politics of Language in African Literature.* Harare: Zimbabwe Publishing House.

Thomas, W. I. 1896. 'The Scope and Method of Folk-Psychology'. *American Journal of Sociology* 1 (4): 434–45.

Thomas, W. I. 1909. 'Standpoint for the Interpretation of Savage Society'. *American Journal of Sociology* 15 (2): 145–63.

Tinsley, Meghan. 2019. 'Decolonizing the Civic/Ethnic Binary'. *Current Sociology* 67 (3): 347–64.

Tuck, Eve, and K. Wayne Yang. 2012. 'Decolonization Is Not a Metaphor'. *Decolonization: Indigeneity, Education & Society* 1 (1): 1–40.

Turner, Bryan S. 1974. 'Islam, Capitalism and the Weber Theses'. *The British Journal of Sociology* 25 (2): 230–43.

Turner, Bryan S. 1978. 'Orientalism, Islam and Capitalism'. *Social Compass* 25 (3–4): 371–94.

Turner, Bryan S. 1989. 'From Orientalism to Global Sociology'. *Sociology* 23 (4): 629–38.

Uys, Tina. 2010. 'Dealing with Domination, Division and Diversity: The Forging of a National Sociological Tradition in South Africa'. In *The ISA Handbook of Diverse Sociological Traditions*, edited by Sujata Patel, 235–45. Los Angeles, CA: SAGE.

Valluvan, Sivamohan. 2019. *The Clamour of Nationalism: Race and Nation in Twenty-First-Century Britain*. Manchester: Manchester University Press.

Vincent, George E. 1896. 'The Province of Sociology'. *American Journal of Sociology* 1 (4): 473–91.

Virdee, Satnam. 2017. 'The Second Sight of Racialised Outsiders in the Imperialist Core'. *Third World Quarterly* 38 (11): 2396–410.

Virdee, Satnam. 2019. 'Racialized Capitalism: An Account of Its Contested Origins and Consolidation'. *The Sociological Review* 67 (1): 3–27.

Wacquant, Loïc. 2008. 'Pierre Bourdieu'. In *Key Sociological Thinkers*, edited by Rob Stones, 2nd edn, 261–77. London: Palgrave Macmillan.

Wacquant, Loïc, and Aksu Akçaoğlu. 2017. 'Practice and Symbolic Power in Bourdieu: The View from Berkeley'. *Journal of Classical Sociology* 17 (1): 55–69.

Wainwright, Steven P. 2011. 'Review Essay: Is Sociology Warming to Climate Change?' *Sociology* 45 (1): 173–7.

Wallace, Derron. 2017. 'Reading "Race" in Bourdieu? Examining Black Cultural Capital Among Black Caribbean Youth in South London'. *Sociology* 51 (5): 907–23.

Walter, Maggie, and Chris Andersen. 2013. *Indigenous Statistics: A Quantitative Research Methodology*. Walnut Creek, CA: Left Coast Press.

Ward, Lester F. 1895. 'The Place of Sociology Among the Sciences'. *American Journal of Sociology* 1 (1): 16–27.

Ward, Lester F. 1903. 'Social Differentiation and Social Integration'. *American Journal of Sociology* 8 (6): 721–45.

Ward, Lester F. 1907. 'Social and Biological Struggles'. *The American Journal of Sociology* 13 (3): 289–99.

Ward, Lester F. 1913. 'Eugenics, Euthenics, and Eudemics'. *American Journal of Sociology* 18 (6): 737–54.

Weatherly, Ulysses G. 1911. 'The Racial Element in Social Assimilation'. *American Journal of Sociology* 16 (5): 593–612.

Weber, Max. 1959. *The Religion of China*. Glencoe, IL: The Free Press.

Weber, Max. 1981. 'Some Categories of Interpretive Sociology'. *Sociological Quarterly* 22 (2): 151–80.

Weber, Max. 2000 [1958]. *The Religion of India*. Glencoe, IL: The Free Press.

Weber, Max. 2001 [1905]. *The Protestant Ethic and the Spirit of Capitalism: And Other Writings*. London: Routledge.

Whyte, Kyle. 2017. 'Indigenous Climate Change Studies: Indigenizing Futures, Decolonizing the Anthropocene'. *English Language Notes* 55 (1): 153–62.

Whyte, Kyle. 2018. 'Indigenous Science (Fiction) for the Anthropocene: Ancestral Dystopias and Fantasies of Climate Change Crises'. *Environment and Planning E: Nature and Space* 1 (1–2): 224–42.

Wilder, Gary. 2004. 'Race, Reason, Impasse: Césaire, Fanon, and the Legacy of Emancipation'. *Radical History Review* 90 (1): 31–61.

Williams, Eric. 1944. *Capitalism and Slavery*. Chapel Hill, NC: University of North Carolina Press.

Wolfe, Patrick. 2006. 'Settler Colonialism and the Elimination of the Native'. *Journal of Genocide Research* 8 (4): 387–409.

Wright, Earl, II. 2002a. 'The Atlanta Sociological Laboratory 1896–1924: A Historical Account of the First American School of Sociology'. *The Western Journal of Black Studies* 26 (3): 165–74.

Wright, Earl, II. 2002b. 'Using the Master's Tools: The Atlanta University and American Sociology, 1896–1924'. *Sociological Spectrum* 22 (1): 15–39.

Wright, Earl, II. 2012. 'Why, Where, and How to Infuse the Atlanta Sociological Laboratory into the Sociology Curriculum'. *Teaching Sociology* 40 (3): 257–70. https://doi.org/10.1177/0092055X12444107.

Wright, Earl, II. 2016. *The First American School of Sociology: W.E.B. Du Bois and the Atlanta Sociological Laboratory*. Farnham: Ashgate.

Wright, Earl, II, and Thomas C. Calhoun. 2012. 'Jim Crow Sociology: Toward an Understanding of the Origin and Principles of Black Sociology via the Atlanta Sociological Laboratory'. *Sociological Focus* 39 (1): 1–18.

Wynter, Sylvia. 2003. 'Unsettling the Coloniality of Being/Power/Truth/Freedom: Towards the Human, After Man, Its Overrepresentation – An Argument'. *CR: The New Centennial Review* 3 (3): 257–337.

Yacine, Tassadit. 2016. 'Pierre Bourdieu in Algeria at War: Notes on the Birth of an Engaged Ethnosociology'. *Ethnography* 5 (4): 487–509.

Young, Robert J. C. 2004. *White Mythologies*. 2nd edn. London: Routledge.

Zeiny, Esmaeil. 2017. 'Spokesmen of Intellectual Decolonization: Shariati in Dialogue with Alatas'. In *Ali Shariati and the Future of Social Theory*, edited by Dustin J. Byrd and Seyed Javad Miri, 64–84. Leiden: Brill.

Zimmerman, Andrew. 2006. 'Decolonizing Weber'. *Postcolonial Studies* 9 (1): 53–79.

Zuberi, Tukufu. 2000. 'Deracializing Social Statistics: Problems in the Quantification of Race'. *The Annals of the American Academy of Political and Social Science* 568 (1): 172–85.

Zuberi, Tukufu. 2001. *Thicker Than Blood: How Racial Statistics Lie*. Minneapolis, MN: University of Minnesota Press.

Zuberi, Tukufu, and Eduardo Bonilla-Silva. 2008. 'Telling the Real Tale of the Hunt: Toward a Race Conscious Sociology of Racial Stratification'. In *White Logic, White Methods: Racism and Methodology*, edited by Tukufu Zuberi and Eduardo Bonilla-Silva, 329–41. Lanham, MD: Rowman & Littlefield.

Index